How to Overcome Anxiety

Effective Ways to Manage Stress, Fears, Panic Attacks and Reclaiming Your Life Again

Amber Wise

Table of Contents

Introduction

The term anxiety finds its direct counterpart in the Latin word a*nxia*, which in turn derives from the Latin verb *ango,* which means "to tighten, suffocate or distress". Therefore, already from the derivation of the term we can understand that anxiety involves states of agitation and mental suffocation in front of possible dangerous situations or uncertainties.

The ancient Greeks, however, called anxiety "melancholy" and believed that it derived from an excess of black bile in the body. For those who don't know what black bile is, it is, according to Hippocratic philosophy, one of the four basic humors. It is described as a cold, dry fluid, generated by the archetype of the earth. To designate these states of "bile", it was usual to use terms such as "anger", or "black humor", which means "melancholy".

This idea that we had an excess of black bile in the body was supported by Hippocrates (460 BC - 377 BC) and later accepted by Aristotle (384 BC - 322 BC). Such black bile was curiously cured with wine, so I will let you imagine how they went crazy with what was considered a natural remedy to physiological symptoms. I have a slightly ironic explanation about why wine was used as a natural remedy. They got drunk and stopped thinking about everything that was afflicting them.

Following this hypothesis, we can say the ancient Greeks were the first to "drink in order to forget". Staying on the subject, currently there are people who when sick or have too many thoughts in their heads get drunk, hoping to forget all their problems, but the drunkenness is temporary and when they wake up from the hangover the problems remain the same. Could they be descendants of the ancient Greeks? Why not?

We have to wait until the Middle Ages (the historical period from 476 AD to 1492) onward for anxiety to be conceived as a mental and spiritual illness. In this era, the cure for anxiety is entrusted to religion, which states that it can remedy anxiety through the redemption of the sins of the person afflicted. From a contemporary perspective, we might liken such a practice to confession to a priest. But if we confess to the priest, do our anxieties and thoughts disappear? The answer is no.

Religion in the Middle Ages was at its peak and offered itself as a cure from all evil. We must not forget that while it was manifesting itself as a cure, for 500 years it persecuted and killed women because they were considered "witches". We must not forget those poor victims. In fact, it is estimated that there were about one million women killed, without any reason, maybe because they had another religion or because they cured diseases with herbs.

This does not take away from the fact that this period of witch inquisition was one of the darkest periods of humanity, and I hope that all of us will never forget all those victims, poor women and mothers of children, who died because they had different cultures or traditions. Now back to us.

During the Enlightenment, on the other hand, medical-biological research began to develop, and many remedies were proposed to fight anxiety using decoctions, bloodletting, opium and precious stones.

These remedies continued to play a fundamental role in the treatment of anxiety states or symptoms of anxiety.

We will have to wait until 1800 to progressively conceive anxiety as a mental illness to be treated with drugs and psychotherapy. But to date, what is anxiety and how does it manifest itself?

What is anxiety and how it manifests

Did you know that approximately 30% of people on the planet will suffer from anxiety disorders in their lifetimes? And did you know that women suffer from these disorders roughly twice as much as men? But what is anxiety and how come, at least once in our lives, we all will suffer from it?

Anxiety is a psychic state characterized by feelings related fear and intense worry, often unjustified. Such anxiety, at times, can be induced by a specific environment to which our organism does not adapt, and therefore to our brains do not respond to adaptation in a given situation; then all this procure an accumulation of stress.

Between anxiety and fear, the differences are minimal and present a very strong link, but they are not the same thing or emotion, as many believe. Fear is more archaic or primitive than anxiety; in fact, it is an emotion we also share with the animal kingdom, especially with regard to "mammals". Anxiety, on the other hand, unlike fear, appears to be a typically human emotion. We invented it and could say that it is an emotion that has developed from fear to allow us to feel more protected. All of this, it is believed, occurred simultaneously as humans were beginning to develop cognitive skills such as imagination, anticipation or foresight, and planning.

In fact, these are the skills according to which our species differs from the animal genus. Anxiety and fear, therefore, act as protection for our species by triggering similar physiological systems and activating in front of threatening stimuli (real or imaginary). If fear makes sense in allowing us to survive, does the same apply to anxiety? Not exactly.

There is a factor that differs from fear and anxiety, and it is a factor upon which we can understand when and how we are affected by fear (I mean the imaginary kind) or anxiety. The factor that differs between the two lies in "how it happens" and "how long it lasts". In other words, when faced with a fearful stimulus, we are frightened "during" the fearful stimulus; this implies that we are present at that moment, and once the threat disappears, the fear disappears.

During anxiety, on the other hand, the situation is a bit different; it is triggered even only by a "perceived" threat, i.e., one not tangible and therefore not real, that cannot be shared with others because we perceive it only ourselves - and very often something very vague or ill-defined can be perceived. In doing so, anxiety involves our ability to predict or anticipate events by projecting into the future and ending up ceasing to be in the present to enjoy life.

Anxiety, therefore, can manifest long before a fearful threat occurs and that fear is not said to occur. It is not said that a threat exists, but we still wait for it to arrive to make us feel protected and defended. We end up totally losing contact with reality or space-time. To summarize this brief introduction to anxiety, anxiety is the emotion that occurs before the threat, while fear accompanies the threat. Or, in terms of space-time, while we experience anxiety we are projected into the future, and who knows where with our mind.

On the other hand, when we experience a fearful stimulus, and therefore are afraid, we are in the "here and now". A practical example of anxiety is when we have an important exam. Already many days before the day of the exam, we start to worry excessively, thus ending up fearing the exam itself and entering into a state of anxiety accompanied by stress.

All this will result in us studying for the exam in an unhealthy way and arriving at the exam with an exaggerated accumulation of stress. If we say that stressful situations allow us to grow, all this can become a problem if the stress generated is not caused by real factors that allow us to grow, but only by our imagination anxiety.

For example, if we are afraid of making a mistake, when we make a mistake, we generate stress; but this will lead to growth as we will have learned where we went wrong and how to improve. In the case of anxiety, this is not the case because we will foresee what might happen; but if it never happens, we will end up with stress generated by the imagination and will not have learned a damn thing because we stood still while the world continued to turn.

With anxiety, we define an emotion accompanied by strong concerns in which we project ourselves into the future or anticipate a dangerous situation or negative event, all accompanied by the physiological stimuli of fear and annoying feelings of being threatened by everything around us. With anxiety, in a nutshell, we don't just project ourselves into the future, we also project ourselves into the worst endings! I would like you to understand that if maybe we start projecting ourselves into the future and the best endings or positive events, in that case from "anxiety", it would become "believing we can do it". But it's not like that; we don't project the best endings, but the worst ones. And our brains reacts to those (imaginary) worse endings as if they were true. They end up blocking us from even trying to approach our fears. The brain does not recognize the difference between what is real and what is not; consequently, it activates all those stimuli that in "normal" situations would be triggered in circumstances that are dangerous for our survival, i.e., in front of stimuli that are scary or risky for our health.

The brain evaluates a dangerous situation even before it is triggered or may occur; for example, we may find ourselves worried about making a phone call because we do not know how the recipient of the call will take it. Consequently, by exaggerating this fear and becoming anxious, we trigger the stimuli that would be triggered in us as if we were in front of angry lions.

Therefore, anxiety has an adaptive function to identify and prepare us for possible future risks. In and of itself, anxiety is not an abnormal phenomenon. It is a basic emotion that involves states of worry. If fear performs a protective task and helps us safeguard our species by helping us in dangerous situations to be more responsive, anxiety is the "power up" of fear. It is triggered before fear, and if fear is triggered in potentially dangerous situations, anxiety seeks to prevent those dangerous situations from existing.

This may seem useful from the evolutionary perspective of humankind, but it is not really so. "Preventing" our fears by projecting ourselves into the future or possible negative scenarios that could happen might seem like a useful thing to do, partly because in this way we can avoid dangerous situations and thus get the "fearful stimuli" - but without danger - because we are anticipating them before they happen.

All this might seem like a useful thing so if we foresee harmful situations, we don't end up in dangerous situations. In reality there is another factor to evaluate: those situations we project in our minds could or could not happen. But our brains "read" those distorted projections, and in 90% of cases, they end up blocked.

One example would be performance anxiety, which some males know a little about. This type of anxiety is triggered when, generally, the fear or excessive and disproportionate concern about a future action gets the better of us and ends up blocking us, perhaps because we believe we cannot do it or are not up to expectations.

In summary, the person afflicted with this type of anxiety (although it is true for all other types) anticipates situations that require a certain performance. They foreshadow catastrophic outcomes, such as the fear of being evaluated negatively, being awkward, inadequate or ready to fail. Performance anxiety, of course, also presents itself with symptoms, such as excessive stress, irritability, and insomnia that increase as you approach the "test". What is perceived physiologically changes from subject to subject.

Back to us. Anxiety manifests itself to prevent situations that could be dangerous or could "limit" us by preventing us from trying for fear of failure. Remember what we said about "the fear of failure"? By not failing, you are denying yourself the opportunity to grow and improve.

But how does anxiety manifest?

On a cognitive level, anxiety manifests with a sense of emptiness on a mental level, with signals and senses of alarm and danger that grow over time, with the induction of negative images, memories or thoughts, with the triggering of protective behaviors, and with the constant feeling of being observed and the center of attention. Some pretty good mental wankers, huh?

At the behavioral level, anxiety is manifested by an induction in the human mind of the tendency to check the surrounding environment and assess whether it is safe or harmful. This ends up making the person feel uncomfortable if the environment is assessed as dangerous even without any apparent reason. In addition, at the behavioral level, it also manifests itself with the continuous search for explanations, reassurance or escape routes. The way of thinking of anxious people we can say, therefore, is: "prevention is better than cure".

Think about it for a moment: what keeps anxiety alive is not the frightening event or the situation we fear in itself, but the thoughts we have about the event or how we prefigure it in our minds (in most cases with negative outcomes). In addition, protective behaviors are not unusual, such as being accompanied everywhere by someone.

On a physical level, anxiety manifests wit: tension, trembling, sweating, palpitations, increased heart rate, dizziness, nausea. tingling in the extremities of our body and around our mouth, derealization and depersonalization. Don't they remind you of the symptoms of fear? I told you that the two emotions belong to the same copper, only that fear is a primary and animal emotion, while anxiety is a purely human emotion.

Chapter 1:
Understanding Anxiety

Here, we will explore and define anxiety, understand its different forms, and consider types of treatment. By the end, you will have an idea of the type of anxiety you are experiencing, how it manifests in your mind and body, and why it is important to take action to treat it.

Your Anxious Mind and Body

Anxiety is defined as the "anticipation of future threat." People with anxiety experience tension, worry about potential threats, and avoid potentially dangerous situations. Let's consider an example as we work through what it means to have anxiety.

Samantha has not left home in six months. When she was employed, she would at least go out daily and maintain a routine. Now, she finds it nearly impossible. Routine activities, like buying groceries, reduce her to tears. She's experienced panic attacks before and is afraid to have them again—so she avoids places that might be triggers. It feels like her whole life revolves around her anxiety, fear, and avoidance.

One rainy day, the doorbell rings while she is home alone, and she feels herself start to panic. Her breathing becomes shallow and her heart starts to race. Instead of going to open the door, she hides in her bedroom until the person leaves. It takes a very long time afterward for her to calm down.

While it seems like Samantha's anxiety is triggered by the doorbell in this situation, the process is a bit more complicated.

Anxiety in Your Brain

An anxiety attack starts with your sensory receptors: eyes, ears, nose. Imagine Samantha hearing the doorbell. Neurons in her brain stem begin to fire more intensely. Neurotransmitters such as norepinephrine send messages to parts of her brain shouting, "Alert, alert!" While a typical response to a ringing doorbell might be one of surprise or excitement and could involve some of the same initial brain processes, Samantha interprets her experience as anxiety, which starts a cycle that increases her level of arousal.

The messages sent to Samantha's brain are received by her amygdala and hippocampus. The amygdala lies deep in the brain, receives incoming signals, and alerts the rest of her brain to threats. It processes feelings, emotions, and fear quickly—without it, you would never feel anxiety.

In contrast, her hippocampus stores threatening experiences in her brain as memories and analyzes incoming threats in terms of past experience. When a threat is sensed, Samantha's hippocampus exchanges messages with other parts of her brain (such as her prefrontal cortex, which is responsible for planning) to decide whether to send a signal for her body to respond.

Anxiety in Your Body

Once Samantha's brain decides to respond, her sympathetic nervous system is stimulated. Adrenaline and other hormones surge through her body. Her heart rate increases, blood pressure rises, and breathing becomes rapid. In the presence of an actual threat, her body is now prepared to fight or escape. Unfortunately for Samantha, there is no real physical threat and anxiety is the result.

Attention! If you're suffering from major depression or having immediate thoughts of suicide or self-harm, put this book down right now and visit your local hospital emergency room or call 911. If you are experiencing other major mental health issues, contact your mental health professional or primary doctor for assistance.

Where Does Anxiety Stem From?

Some people have anxious feelings all through their entire lives; others do not experience anxiety until after an event or trauma triggers it. Anxiety is thought to result from a combination of factors that differs for each person. Genetics are thought to play a role, as are aspects of your early development.

Have your family members ever been diagnosed with anxiety? Twin studies are used to determine the role of genetics in anxiety disorders since identical twins share the same genes. A 2001 study of twin studies in the American Journal of Psychiatry found that genetics contributes 30 to 40 percent toward the cause of anxiety disorders. This means that anxiety tends to run in families, and you are more likely to develop an anxiety disorder if someone in your family already has one.

Environmental factors are also thought to play a role in anxiety. Events during childhood such as abuse or an overly critical parent may trigger anxiety. Life events that most people experience, such as moving, relationship problems, and loss of loved ones, may trigger anxiety in those already at risk due to their genetics. Having an anxious parent can make you more likely to develop a problem with anxiety yourself because you learn from watching your parent and eventually develop the same patterns of behavior.

Specific phobias, such as the fear of flying, often have a quick onset: a situation that formerly did not cause you anxiety or discomfort suddenly becomes a source of fear. In this case, a sensitizing event such as bad turbulence on a flight may be the trigger. If you are already predisposed toward anxiety, your mind may have difficulty letting go of the memory of the event and cause you to be on guard for similar future threats.

The Anxiety/Fear Connection

The DSM-5 defines fear as an "emotional response to real or perceived imminent threat." When does fear run off the rails and become anxiety?

Fear can help alert us to danger but becomes anxiety when it is out of proportion to the situation. Feeling afraid about giving a public speech is natural. Most people do it anyway, learn that it is not dangerous, and feel less fear. In contrast, a person at risk for anxiety might feel such intense fear that, for example, avoiding public speaking seems necessary. Once avoided, the fear is lessened, and the person mistakenly thinks public speaking is the problem. Fear is no longer warning about danger; instead, the anxiety is causing distress.

Forms of Anxiety

Anxiety is not a one-size-fits-all disorder; it can manifest in many different ways. Below are five types of anxiety disorders. In each case, an anxiety disorder is only diagnosed when fear causes significant impairment in life and has been present for many months.

- **SPECIFIC PHOBIA**

People with specific phobias fear objects or situations such as animals or heights. Most phobias are about things most people fear; however, the fear or anxiety is out of proportion to the actual danger in those with anxiety. A person with a fear of dogs might find it impossible to visit friends who own dogs. Someone with a fear of needles might avoid receiving important medical care. Specific phobias are diagnosed when the fear has a severe impact on a person's life over a period of several months.

- **SOCIAL ANXIETY DISORDER**

People with social anxiety disorder (SAD) have an intense fear of being embarrassed or judged during social or performance situations like going to a party or giving a speech. They may fear blushing, shaking, or acting in ways that will make others think they are strange or anxious.

- **PANIC DISORDER**

Panic disorder involves intense, unexpected episodes of panic with physical symptoms such as a racing heart, shortness of breath, chest pain, and dizziness. When these attacks first happen, the person may attribute them to a medical cause and visit the hospital looking for help. People with panic disorder may feel they are going crazy and worry about having more attacks.

- **AGORAPHOBIA**

People with agoraphobia fear being in situations where escape or receiving help would be difficult if they were to have a panic attack, like in a crowded theater. In these situations, they may think: "What happens if I panic and can't leave?" Some people with agoraphobia feel better with a trusted friend or relative, while others stop leaving home completely. Most people with agoraphobia have lived with their fear for six months or longer.

- GENERALIZED ANXIETY DISORDER

Generalized anxiety disorder (GAD) involves intense, chronic worry. People with GAD worry about health, finances, family members, having an accident—nearly everything. When one worry goes away, another takes its place. This type of worry persists over many months and is often accompanied by physical symptoms.

You Can Get Better

Trying cognitive behavioral therapy or other treatments for the first time can be daunting, especially if you feel you've tried everything and nothing has worked. Unraveling anxiety might feel like you're exposing yourself to more pain. However, the outcome is worth it. Below is a list of ways that overcoming anxiety will change your life.

- Your life goals will be easier to achieve. When you are no longer fearful and avoiding situations, you will feel free to pursue that promotion or take that once-in-a-lifetime trip. Goals that seemed out of reach will suddenly become realistic.
- You will think more positively about your future. Anxiety tends to cast a negative outlook on what is yet to come. When you are free of anxiety, you will feel more hopeful about what is around the next corner.
- It will be easier to cope with medical conditions. You won't

worry unnecessarily about your physical health, but rather will do what is necessary to take care of yourself. Visits to the doctor will no longer fill you with anxiety and dread.

- You may feel relief from depression or low mood. When anxiety is relieved, depression and low mood often show improvement as well. Along with feeling less anxious, you may feel more optimistic, have more energy, sleep better, and generally have more interest in life.

- Anxiety will no longer define you as a person. If you have long-held beliefs about yourself that center around being anxious, those will be replaced with feelings of self-esteem and self-worth. You will get to know the person you can be without those anxious thoughts.

- You will take better care of yourself. Overcoming anxiety will shed light on areas of your life that have been neglected. You will give more importance to things like nutrition, exercise, and being present in the moment.

- Relationships and work that have suffered will improve. You might develop new social connections or feel less dependent on the people you have leaned on in the past. Your increased ability to concentrate will make work seem like less of a chore, and you might even find yourself seeking advancement in the workplace.

- You will feel increased enjoyment in life and more confidence. Anxiety has a way of zapping your confidence and happiness. If you've felt like every day that you are just "getting through," you will now start each day confidently and in search of joy.

Chapter 2:
Determining Your Type of Anxiety

There are five main types of anxiety disorders, all of which involve certain types of anxiety, and there are different ways it can be triggered and addressed. Cognitive behavioral therapy (CBT) is considered by many mental health professionals as the preferred psychosocial intervention for most of them.

In addition to its impressive effectiveness, it also helps the individual to lead a better life even with the disorder. It teaches him many valuable skills to help him deal with his conditions. Listed below are some of the anxiety disorders and how CBT can help people overcome each.

Generalized Anxiety Disorder (GAD)

One of the most prevalent anxiety disorders, Generalized Anxiety Disorder (GAD) is characterized by excessive concern for almost everything in a person's life without a particular cause or reason.

People who have GAD tend to have a big problem with everything. They become anxious about everything in their life, be it their financial status, work, family, friends, or health. They are always worried about the worry that something terrible may happen. They expect the worst-case scenario above all and always try to see things from a negative point of view.

That said, it is easy to see how GAD can make it difficult for someone to live a happy and healthy life. It can be an obstacle to your daily life and become a problem regarding your work, family, friends, and any other social activity. Some of the most common symptoms of GAD include worry or excessive tension, tiredness, inability to rest, difficulty sleeping, headaches, mood swings, difficulty concentrating, and nausea.

Yoga has been shown to help reduce a person's stress, which in turn relaxes their muscles. There are several different yoga poses and routines that you can find online designed to relieve your stress and anxiety. Some examples include eagle pose, head pose, child pose, crescent pose, and legs.

By using CBT, a person with GAD will have a much more favorable outlook on life. Rather than always worrying and thinking about the worst-case scenario, CBT reinforces an optimistic and reasonable outlook on life, which will then have a positive impact on your behavior. Most of the time, they change from a tense and nervous person to a relaxed and calm person who does not assume the worst of everything.

Social Anxiety

Another common type of anxiety is social anxiety, characterized by immediate distress when you meet or interact with unknown people. Affecting more than 15 million different American adults can be considered one of the most prominent types of anxiety in the country.

Also known as "social phobia," people with social anxiety often show visible signs or symptoms that indicate their discomfort towards the situation. Some of those symptoms may include flushing, stuttering, increased heart rate, sweating, being uncomfortable or bored, and, in the worst case, experiencing a full-blown anxiety attack.

If you are one of the many people who suffer from social anxiety, you would understand how much of a disturbance it can have in your life. Because it prevents you from many social interactions, you may have difficulty connecting with other people and making new friends. This can affect your personality and prevent you from having fun when hanging out with friends as you don't dare to stand up and speak for yourself. You are afraid to get involved in social situations and do everything possible to stay hidden and avoid interacting with other people at all costs.

Look at the current situation you are facing. Describe it to yourself. Evaluate how that particular situation made you feel and identify those feelings.

Assess your thoughts about that particular scenario and explore what your mind thought immediately when you faced that situation. The first thoughts that appear in your head are your "automatic thoughts."

Panic Disorder

Panic attacks are characterized by unexpected emotions or feelings of fear when, in fact, there is no real reason to be afraid. Having recurring panic attacks for no apparent reason is what is known as panic disorder. This is mostly found in young adults aged 20 and older. However, it can also be experienced by other children who also have panic symptoms.

Anxiety disorders can significantly affect a person's life. Always being at risk for spontaneous panic attacks can lead them to avoid going out and therefore isolate themselves from others. People with panic disorder generally live in fear of having another panic attack, so they do their best to control it or even hide from other people.

People with panic disorder often spend most of their time fearing the possibility of another panic attack (a fear known as "agoraphobia"). Agoraphobia is when people remain on high alert for possible panic attacks and always keep their guard up in the event of real danger. This can lead them to avoid certain places like shopping malls, festivals, cinemas, supermarkets, and the like.

Several CBT techniques can help people with panic disorder overcome their condition or calm each time a panic attack arises. Developing your calming skills is one of the most remarkable methods. If you are struggling with panic disorder, try this essential guide to ease your mind and prevent a panic attack from escalating once you feel anxiety knocking on your mind's door.

Obsessive-Compulsive Disorder

Obsessive-compulsive disorder, also known as OCD, is a psychological problem that involves uncontrollable ideas or thought patterns and behaviors that you feel compelled or have a sudden need to do. These are unwanted thoughts, obsessions, or images that enter the individual's mind and can serve as a significant discomfort that will essentially become an obstacle between the individual's daily activities and mentality. Subsequently, the individual will have no choice but to participate or perform repetitive acts and behaviors to control or deal with these thoughts.

OCD can significantly affect one's lifestyle. With these thoughts and compulsions, they will stop their daily activities and try to get involved or manage their feelings. This type of mental problem can start at age seven and progress later. Generally, affecting boys over women, the rate of people with OCD will increase more on the women's side in the long term. There are different types of obsessions and compulsions when it comes to OCD.

It can have a significant impact on your school, work, social, and personal life. This may allow them to have difficulty falling asleep, maintaining hygiene, forming friends, maintaining their grades, or participating in any type of social or sports performance.

There are different types of symptoms when it comes to OCD. Cognitive symptoms include continually thinking, "I am responsible for everything," "What if I get sick from this?" and "I must know everything!"

Physical symptoms such as muscle tension, constant stomach pain, dizziness, headaches, and feeling disconnected from your body can also be identified. For further implication that an individual has this type of psychological problem, there are emotional symptoms that you can also check, such as anxiety, sadness, guilt, shame, and anger.

CBT tries to replace your unwanted thoughts and images with positive images to gain a much more positive outlook on life. Positive thoughts will lead to positive emotions that are likely to produce better behaviors towards situations after working on the cognitive side. This can allow them to control how they react to specific scenarios and manage their compulsion.

There are also some helpful CBT techniques that individuals may use whenever they feel those unwanted images creeping at their doorstep again or if they become unsettled by the emotions they're having. One of those techniques is to find the root cause of your thoughts and feelings.

Post-Traumatic Stress Disorder

Post-traumatic stress disorder (PTSD) is a type of anxiety disorder that stems from traumatic, stressful, or terrifying events that can lead a person to experience traumatic episodes that force them to relive that same event.

PTSD is known to have a significant effect on people's lives. This can prevent them from trying things, going to different places, or socializing with other people regularly. A traumatic event (such as a car accident or natural calamity) can make people always think about that occasion and experience horrible setbacks, as well as nightmares. People with PTSD tend to avoid things that remind them of that experience. So every time they see a trigger, they experience panic attacks or flashbacks. This can prevent them from experiencing other things and will eventually isolate them from others.

This type of anxiety disorder should be treated as soon as possible to relieve the psychological distress and avoid any long-term damaging effects. Symptoms of post-traumatic stress disorder include recurring memories of a specific traumatic experience, constant nightmares about it, and terrifying negative thoughts related to it. Along with this, people with PTSD also experience rapid heart rates, profuse sweating, anxiety, and sometimes emotional numbness.

One of the best treatments recommended by therapists is cognitive-behavioral therapy. CBT helps people overcome trauma and eliminate negative thoughts about that scenario and replace them with positive ones that help them sleep better at night. It can also change how they react to a particular object, situation, or person that could trigger their PTSD. Trauma-focused CBT can use a variety of techniques that will help people triumph over this mental disorder and find other, healthier, and more positive outlets to direct their energy.

Overcoming Anxiety

Most anxiety is caused because your thoughts are either fixated on bad events from the past or else focused too much on the future. You can do a lot to help your anxiety by grounding your thoughts in the present only. By focusing on the present, you will stop dwelling on things you can't change in the past and you stop worrying about things that may never even happen in the future.

But if fixating on the past or present is a habit, you may wonder how you can ground yourself in the present more. Thinking in the present is certainly a healthy habit that will take some mental effort to achieve. One thing that can help you is trying mindfulness.

There is another huge benefit to mindfulness. Mindfulness makes you aware of your thoughts. That enables you to control them better, which helps you overcome and break poor mental habits. Mindfulness is really just the habit of being totally aware of your current existence. You maintain awareness of what is going on around you and in your mind. This may sound relatively simple, but if you think about it, you spend a lot of time with your mind drifting away from your present surroundings, and you probably have very little consciousness or control over your thoughts until they enter your mind, seemingly out of the blue. You are more preoccupied with your worries, plans, and daydreams than your current existence. Therefore, becoming mindful can be a bit of a challenge. It is a new form of awareness and a new style of thinking that you must develop. Essentially, it is an important skill that you must master.

It is also helpful to think about those times in your life when you were truly mindful without trying. There are probably some moments when you got so into what was presently happening that you shut out all worries and other distractions. Sex, fun, and deep conversation are examples of times when you might become mindful. Now, imagine reliving those moments right now. Try to capture that feeling again and apply it to your current situation. Try to feel that way all over again. The more you relive that feeling of being mindful in your memory, the more your mind will get used to the sensation. Soon, the state of being mindful will become more normal. You will be able to achieve the feeling and the focus instantly, at will.

Love can help encourage you to be mindful, as well. When you are engaged in an activity that brings you true enjoyment, you find that you are willing to become absorbed in that activity. It is important to do things that you enjoy. This adds zest to your life and gives you a reason to keep moving forward. Take time for yourself and do something you really love. It does not matter what it is, as long as it is not something harmful, like taking drugs or hurting yourself in any way. Healthy, meaningful activities are what keep you sane and add joy to your days. You are miserable enough with your anxiety and depression; why deprive yourself of fun activities and the things you genuinely enjoy?

It can be hard to clear time in your schedule to practice mindfulness. But it is important that you practice it. Just a few minutes a day is sufficient. When you are about to go to bed is a great time to engage in lengthier meditations. You will find that practicing mindfulness meditation before bed will help you sleep more soundly because it helps you turn off your restless brain and just focus on relaxation. A quiet mind is what you need for sleep, but often anxiety prevents you from achieving that level of mental quietness.

I do not recommend using physical activity for mindfulness right before bed, however, as this will only increase your energy level and heart rate, making sleep harder. Calming exercise like yoga or Tai Chi can be great before bed, but only if you practice a routine designed for bringing about sleep.

Chapter 3:
Practicing Mindfulness to Overcome Anxiety

Mindfulness is one of the most helpful tools for all forms of mental illness. Whether you are anxious all the time, or just experience social anxiety in situations with other people around, you can benefit from mindfulness. It can be helpful for those that have constant depressive thoughts as well.

It can be easy to run away with your thoughts when you are feeling stressed and overwhelmed. You might escape to a place in your mind, real or not, where you don't have to think about the present. It might be a fantasy of a life that's better than the one you are living, or perhaps you often reminisce on times that were better than now.

Mindfulness is the attempt to ground you and keep you in reality, rather than lost in your anxious and stressful thoughts. When you think of one anxious thing, it can easily lead to many other worries. For example, you might think, "Oh no, I have to pay the cable bill because it is already late." Then you might start thinking of all the other bills stacking up, not to mention the debt that's increasing in interest.

Then you start to think about how you aren't making enough money at your current job, or that you should have gone to school for a different subject, or you shouldn't have broken up with that guy who's now a doctor. One thought about a late cable bill can lead to an existential crisis if you don't stop anxiety right in its tracks. Mindfulness will help you through this. Instead of ruminating on what could have, would have, or should have been, you instead focus on the now, which is really what is most important.

It is something that needs to be practiced. You might only be able to be comfortably mindful for a few seconds at a time before your thoughts go straight back to something else. When you find that you are losing yourself in your own thoughts, you have to make sure that you redirect. Back to the example of the cable bill, you might notice your anxiety rising when you think of the other bills stacking up. That is when you would stop your thoughts and instead use a mindful tactic to bring you back to the present and instead focus on the cable bill.

Then, you might find that your mind is wandering again, and before you know it, you are thinking about that wealthy guy and what could have been. You have not failed, but you just need to redirect again, either using a new mindful technique or just practicing the other one again. Don't punish yourself for drifting back into those thoughts.

Picture yourself driving down a highway. The present is the road in front of you, the past the grass to the right, and the future the other road on the left. If you drift too far right or left, then you'll get lost and off track. Mindfulness is what's going to keep you moving forward in the right direction. At first, you are going to be driving down the road very wobbly. Every time you feel yourself drift off to the right or the left, redirect and focus back on going straight. Eventually, you'll find it very easy to avoid drifting at all.

Mindfulness should be practiced whenever you are experiencing symptoms of anxiety. You should practice mindfulness even when you aren't in a negative mindset. Maybe you are just bored or restless, which are also forms of anxiety. We don't always view being bored as a bad thing, and many people feel lucky if they get the chance to have nothing to occupy their time. If you are bored for too long, however, you might find your thoughts drifting somewhere dangerous, so practice mindfulness even if you don't feel like you are that obviously anxious.

Even if you aren't feeling totally anxious, you can still use these to help prevent future moments of anxiety. No harm will come from mindfulness. These aren't the only methods of mindfulness either.

Some activities would be considered mindful, such as playing a game or reading a book. Anything that keeps your mind on the present is going to be mindful. We might not always have the time to play a game or read a book to pull us out of our thoughts, however, so it is important to remember to use these tools for when you are feeling anxious.

Five Senses

Your five senses are your ability to see, smell, taste, hear, and touch. When being mindful, a good practice is to go through each of these senses to feel better. This activity starts by sitting somewhere comfortably, preferably with your feet flat on the floor. When you are in a comfortable place, it is easier for your mind to focus on what it needs to. You might be feeling anxious at work, waiting at the doctor's office, or just in your own home. No matter where you are, you can go through this process to help ground you and keep you in the moment, avoiding anxious and depressive automatic thoughts.

First is your sight. Find five things that you can see. This is just simply anything that is in your range of eyesight. It might be the rug that your feet are on or the building you see out the window. Perhaps it is the table with things sitting on them and all the stuff that's on top. Whatever your five items are, it doesn't matter. The only thing you have to do is identify them.

Next, identify four things that you can smell. Don't actually get up from where you are sitting to smell them. Just try to pick them out. Maybe it is the coffee sitting on the counter or a manhole you see walking down the street. Perhaps you imagine smelling the cat, or the candy sitting in the dish on the table.

Look for three things to touch - easily identifiable things. It might include the couch you are sitting on, your own hair, or your pants. Maybe it is just something across the room, like a salt lamp, or a soft scarf hanging on the coat rack. You don't have to touch these things either. Just think about what three things you could touch.

Find two things you could hear. This could include the birds chirping outside or the music softly playing on the elevator. Perhaps it is the tapping of someone else's foot or the sound of nails scraping on a table. Whatever these are, pick them out.

Pick out one thing that you can taste. This isn't something that has to be edible either. Maybe it is the taste of the water from a fountain in front of you or a sandwich someone else is eating. No matter what it is, everything has a flavor, edible or not, and your goal is to just identify that taste.

You don't actually have to do these activities. You don't have to taste something or smell something. But identifying it as something that you could use that for can be enough to pull you back into the moment. You don't have to go in that order either. Instead, you can try finding five things to touch, four things to hear, three things to taste, two things to smell, and one thing to see. Just remember your five senses and a descending amount.

If you don't have one of these senses, such as the ability to hear, see, or taste, then simply replace that with another sense. Either way, the goal is to give you something you can identify in the moment so that you are pulled away from the anxious thoughts in the first place.

Finding Colors

Another activity for mindfulness is to search for one specific color. When you are feeling anxious, think of one color. It shouldn't be something specific at first, just simply pick something like blue, black, gray, white, or yellow.

Look around the room and pick out everything that is that color. This doesn't have to be done in any specific order. Simply look for things that are red, or green, or any other simple color. Again, if you don't have this ability and are color blind, try using a different "rule." Maybe you find only things that are made of metal, or you pick out all the things made of wood.

Identify what might be a close sister of that color. After picking out all the green stuff, look at that specifically and think about what's lime green, what's forest green, and everything in between.

Before you know it, your mind is on something completely different than what was making you anxious. There are no rules to this either. If you miss an item, nothing bad will happen. The goal is to get your brain to stop thinking about what's causing anxiety and instead look directly toward what's around you at the current moment.

If it isn't working at first, try repeating with a different color. Do this after you do the five senses, or vice versa. Come up with your own games too, like identifying all the things that make white noise, or the things that you can smell that are made of wood. The only thing you have to make sure you are doing is that you are focusing on the now and not on the past or future.

Muscle Relaxation

When we're anxious, it can be hard to realize just how much we might be using our muscles. Your back, jaw, neck, shoulders, and other parts of your body responsible for support can be sore, often because you don't properly manage your anxiety. There are even some people who believe certain pains are associated with certain issues, such as lower back and hip pain being caused by money issues. This isn't proven by science, but it is interesting to think about just how much pain we might be feeling simply because of our anxiety.

Tensing and releasing your muscles is a good form of mindfulness that keeps you focused on the now and will help your body feel better afterward too. It involves identifying your muscles and tensing them for three to five seconds, then holding for one to two seconds in between, focusing on deep breathing the entire time. Don't push yourself if it is too straining and skip over any muscles that might be sore or parts of your body with too much nerve damage. The point isn't to strain yourself, but to focus instead on how tense you are and to relieve that tension.

Start with your head. Clench your jaw for a few seconds and then release. Raise your ears and hold them tight or tilt your neck to each side for a few seconds. Move down to your shoulders, raising them up as high as possible and then dropping them as much as you can. Just when you think you have relaxed your shoulders, relax them even more.

Now, move onto your chest and arms. Hold them tight for a few seconds, releasing for a few afterward. The entire time, make sure that you are fully breathing in and out so you don't lose your breath. Then, go to your stomach, legs, feet, and repeat if you need to. It is not supposed to be a workout, but just a way for you to become aware of how tense you might be. Our muscles can become very sore if we don't hold them properly.

Between each of these muscle tightening moments, make sure to take a deep breath in and let it out slowly. Count your breathing and count how long you are holding. Consistency will help regulate your heart and lungs so that those too help with overall anxiety reduction.

This is why exercising can be so relaxing for many people. It gets your mind focused on something else and keeps the blood pumping. Remember that exercise is healthy and important, but it can also be a source of anxiety. Don't put pressure on yourself to be physical right away, especially if that's one of your triggers. The gym can be a scary place, and even walking down the street can cause people to panic, so while it is important to keep your body moving to avoid anxious symptoms, don't make yourself feel bad that you aren't in a place where you can do this.

Chapter 4:

How to Use Breathing Techniques to Stop Anxiety

Breathing exercises can be a quick way to center yourself before you enter an anxiety-inducing situation or just to calm down when you're feeling anxious. They're also helpful when preparing to meditate. Breathing is a symbol of consistency that we carry with us everywhere. Our breath grounds us and is a shared experience with everyone around us. If you find your anxiety building up and start feeling as if you're lacking control over your thoughts and emotions, remind yourself that your breath is a steady, supportive presence.

Use your breath in times of stress as a reminder that you're never alone. Your breath is always with you, and you have the power to slow it down, listen to it, and use it for comfort.

One of the easiest ways to bring awareness to the breath is to identify the type of breath you're taking. For example, does your breath feel "shallow" or "deep"? A shallow breath is a breath that only reaches your chest and oxygen only reaches the top of your lungs, which results in less oxygen being transported to the rest of your body. You want to support your body with adequate oxygen, which means you want to practice breathing more deeply.

Place a hand on your heart and a hand on your stomach. Take a few breaths and see which hand moves more. If you are breathing deeply and filling your abdomen with oxygen, the hand on your stomach will rise and fall the greatest amount.

The breath connects every part of the body. It regulates heart rate, blood pressure, oxygen levels, and digestion. It assists the body in communicating with the brain and vice versa. This is why breathing exercises are such a great step toward managing social anxiety. When your sympathetic nervous system is triggered by your anxiety, your body might develop a "mind of its own." By taking control of your breath, you're signaling your body to listen and relax.

If You Only Have 5 Minutes

LISTEN TO YOUR BREATH

One of the most important first steps in beginning a meditation practice is to bring focus and awareness to your breath. If your anxiety is building, tuning in to your breathing may help you quickly relieve your symptoms. Follow these steps:

1. Ground yourself in a stable position by sitting in a chair or standing with your feet hip-width apart.

2. With your mouth closed, breathe in deeply through your nose, paying close attention to how the breath feels. Listen to it moving into your body. Then, breathe out through your nose, again paying close attention to how it feels and sounds.

3. On your next breath, breathe in for three slow counts, hold your breath for three slow counts, and release for three slow counts. Be attentive to the way your body moves as you breathe in and out.

4. On your next breath, imagine that you're breathing in positive energy, light, or pleasant images. As you exhale, imagine that you're pushing out negative thoughts or emotions from your body. Repeat the visualization until the five minutes are up.

Upon concluding this exercise, check in with yourself. What did you notice about your physiological reaction? How does your heart rate feel? Throughout the day, it helps to remember that your breath and body are connected. Take a moment now to contemplate how efficiently your blood transports the oxygen you inhale throughout your entire body. Remember, this oxygen fuels you for every situation you encounter.

Using Affirmations During Meditation

Affirmations are statements that when repeatedly regularly help reinforce positive beliefs. For example, if you struggle with a lack of confidence in social situations, spend a few moments repeating to yourself, I'm strong and confident when interacting with other people. Affirmations help create new thought patterns and beliefs that can positively influence your behavior and comfort level in social situations.

You might find the following affirmations useful for channeling your focus toward positive thoughts during meditation. You can use one or a combination to personalize your practice.

- I am worthy of happiness.

- I am unique and beautiful.

- I deserve respect.

- I listen to my heart.

- I deserve to have my voice heard.

- I am capable of sharing love.

- I believe in myself.

- I'm intelligent.

- I trust my feelings.

- I'm a strong, independent individual.

- I deserve peace of mind.

- I'm enough.

Take a few moments to come up with a few affirmations that resonate with you at the present moment. Maybe you're going through a particularly challenging time at work right now or your patience is being tested at home by one of your family members. Whatever the case may be, craft a few affirmations that speak to your heart to help you deal with that particular situation. Also identify other situations in which your anxiety usually manifests and create specific affirmations for those occasions as well.

Once you have a few well-crafted affirmations that feel good to you, practice repeating them out loud or in your head throughout the day. You might consider looking at yourself in a mirror and saying them to yourself. You can also use them when you're meditating. For example, if your mind wanders to negative thoughts, bring your attention back to the meditation by repeating one of your affirmations. Hopefully, in time, you'll begin to believe what you're saying. Just keep at it.

SILENCING YOUR INNER CRITIC

Your inner critic is the one that's always pointing out that what you just did is totally wrong or, at the very least, not quite right. The one that sometimes shouts, sometimes whines, sometimes whispers—but always with the same basic message: you are just not quite up to par. You're flawed, and it's embarrassing. What's wrong with you?! When you notice that your inner critic starts taking center stage in your mind, take a quick 10-minute break to practice this self-compassion meditation.

1. Find a quiet place where you can comfortably sit without distraction, such as the meditation space you identified earlier.

2. Take a deep breath, and settle in. Rest one hand over your heart then place the other on your belly. Say "ahh" to release the tension in your jaw. Breathe.

3. Allow the voice of the inner critic to arise. Allow the emotions that it triggers to arise. Can you experience the emotions as simply bursts of life-force energy? Can you hear the inner critic's words as simply sound—a kind of music like a Mozart string quartet, just not quite as harmonious? If so, great. If not, no problem. Simply notice and allow the thoughts and emotions to be, like the sky allowing clouds space to float.

4. Now offer words of kindness and compassion to yourself. The inner critic is just one member of the committee. Now it's time to give the floor to your inner advocate: the one who offers

words of support. You write the script, and you step into that role. Even better, let it be your "wisdom mind" that's speaking. You know how to do it. Say, "I love you unconditionally." Say, "You are primordially pure." Say, "No human being is perfect, and I love and accept you just the way you are."

When your 10 minutes are up, notice how you feel. Do you feel more compassionate toward yourself? Can you remember to remind yourself from time to time how much you truly do love and accept yourself? If you can make this a habit, you'll feel yourself softening around the edges and may find that some of your social anxiety is easing up.

Don't Try to Force the Benefits

Sometimes when you enter into a new activity such as a meditation practice or breathing exercises, with the wrong mind-set and/or not enough information, you can do more harm than good. Consider the scenario in which you chose to attend a meditation class with your friend. Although your initial goal was to reduce your anxiety through meditation, it actually ended up increasing it in this scenario. Your thoughts ran amok, and you immediately assumed there was something wrong with you.

This fed a negative core belief such as "I'm not good enough," which resulted in more anxiety and discomfort. The negative core belief was reinforced. If you selected the first choice in that scenario, your anxiety escalated to the point where you chose to leave the class in an unhappy state. This might have turned you off from meditation entirely. Had you felt an urgency to "get it right," you likely would have been equally disappointed.

Meditation and breathing exercises are not about meeting a specific goal or experience. Instead, they're giving you an opportunity to simply be present in the moment. So be aware of your state of mind when you're trying these activities. If you hear yourself starting to think "should" statements or feeling as if you're doing something wrong, just pause and bring your awareness back to your breath. Remind yourself that you're giving yourself the gift of developing a new skill, and it will take time to overcome some of your knee-jerk reactions.

If You Have 30 Minutes

MOVE PAST ROADBLOCKS

When living with social anxiety, you might spend a lot of time thinking about a painful memory from your past, because the socially anxious mind has a habit of replaying such scenarios over and over again. This 30-minute meditation practice will help you move past this incident, enjoy the present, and focus on a positive future.

1. Find a quiet place where you can comfortably sit without distraction, such as the meditation space you identified earlier.

2. Close your eyes and bring awareness to your breath. Pay attention to how your breathing affects your heart rate.

3. Scan your body in a manner that allows you to connect with every area of your physical being. Relax your muscles, particularly those in your face, neck, and shoulders, to bring your body to a comfortable resting place.

4. Imagine that you're standing on a pathway in a heavily wooded area. The trees are tall and thick and line the pathway in front of you. Spend a few moments breathing in the crisp, forest air and listening to any sounds you hear.

5. When you're ready, visualize yourself walking down this path, taking note of everything around you. As thoughts or worries enter your mind, simply observe them and bring your awareness back to the wooded path.

6. Now, imagine that you come across several large stones in your pathway. Each stone represents a painful memory from your past. Take a moment to closely observe each stone, identifying the memory and focusing on how everything is concentrated within this hard, solid stone.

7. Select one of the stones and pick it up. Feel the weight of this memory in your palms.

8. When you're ready, turn and place the stone off the pathway, nestled within plants and other rocks. Stand back and appreciate that the stone looks more at home in its new resting place than it did on your path.

9. Do again steps 7 and 8 as many times as you need to until all the stones in your path have been cleared away.

10. Continue walking along the path, observing that up ahead is a brightly lit clearing. If you encounter any other stones, or memories, along the path as you move forward, repeat steps 7 and 8.

11. As you approach the clearing, start to feel the warmth of the bright light. Step into that warmth and breathe in the sunlight as it embraces you.

12. Spend a moment appreciating the sunlight, imagining that it represents all your strength and potential. Remain in this clearing for as long as you like and feel free to explore the area. When you feel ready, bring your awareness back to your breath.

13. Listen to the sound of your breath entering and exiting your body, while wiggling your toes and fingers. Take a moment to appreciate yourself for taking the time to practice meditation. When you're ready, open your eyes.

You may find yourself feeling energized after completing a longer meditation session or you may feel a little drained. Either way, take a few minutes to check in with yourself to notice how you feel, physically, emotionally, and mentally following this meditation. Make observations, but try to avoid judging your experience.

Chapter 5:
How to Manage Your Thoughts to Control Anxiety

We are NOT our mind. Our mind is active and busy — all the time. Here are just a few examples of our mind's activities:

- I can't recall the name of someone and so hours later it "pops" into my mind.

- I awake with memories of a fascinating dream, even though I was sound asleep and made no conscious effort to direct my thoughts.

- I'm listening to a lecture, and suddenly I don't recall anything from the last few minutes because I was lost in my thoughts (daydreaming).

- I am waiting for the physician to return to the exam room and notice my body is tense as I imagine her long syringe and all the pain to follow.

- I'm trying to concentrate on what I'm reading, but all I can think about is the contentious conversation I just had with my partner.

There are many ways in which we can recognize the constant activity of the mind. Our brain is an organ that never turns off. As reflected in some of the examples above, we have conscious thought and unconscious thought, as well. In addition, both types of thoughts can foster and feed anxiety.

We need to recognize that thoughts are thoughts, they are not real.

We also need to recognize that thoughts can be distorted, erroneous, and unhealthy.

Let's tackle the first point:

Thoughts Are Thoughts. They Are Not Real

I will illustrate this point with a common experience in which we get so into our thoughts that they become real to us and have real effects upon our body.

I went to see the Tom Hanks movie, Captain Phillips, in the theater. I knew the true story it was based on, and I understood that I was watching a movie. Even though the film is based upon a true-life story, it was not actually occurring at the moment. What was actually occurring was that I was sitting in a comfortable theater seat, having some buttery popcorn and a soda. My conscious mind knows this, but I got pulled into the movie and soon I was reacting to this cinematic event like it was real. I tense up and show emotion in reaction to the scenes (and the reactions of those around me). It is all very real, except it isn't.

Similar to an experience in a theater, we get caught up in the movies playing in our mind as though they were real. We recall and relive past events, what was said, what should have been said, what would be said the next time, etc. If the event was particularly unpleasant or stressful, we can actually feel those emotions returning. We imagine tough questions, or negative reactions, or negative feelings and before we know it, we are feeling the same negative emotions as though in present reality.

Sometimes, merely anticipating an anxiety-inducing situation can take us into that theater of the mind. Individuals with anxiety about crowds may park outside a venue anticipating the crush of the crowd, worried there might be familiar faces inside, and begin to physically react. Their body tenses and their breathing become shallow.

Our thoughts are NOT real, but we can get caught up in our thoughts, which causes very real effects on our body.

How to use this information:

1. Being able to recognize that your thoughts are separate from you gives some degree of detachment. It is a starting point for learning to observe your thoughts rather than become your thoughts. Once you can create some distance from your thoughts, you can talk to yourself about those thoughts rather than letting your automatic, negative thoughts do all the talking (and directing).

2. Remind yourself that these negative thoughts are your mind repeating its endless activity and that they are only thoughts. Your mind has repetitive thoughts and it seems almost as though the initial mental response (habit) for many people is a negative response. Our thoughts can be powerfully negative. They do not have power over you unless you get lost in them and treat them as real, giving up your power to be present in the moment.

3. Tune in to what is real. Use the power of your mind in a positive way by directing it toward what is real. Don't let your

thoughts run the show; become the director. A great way to do this is to direct your mind and tune into the five senses of your body. Become aware of the immediate, real world around you by opening up your senses. Notice your immediate surroundings through your senses. If you notice what is real and, in the moment, in most case you have nothing to worry about. If there is something to worry about, then do something about it. In other words, if there is a real, live response necessary to the moment, then do it. If not, let go of the thoughts and tune in and observe the moment.

4. Let your thoughts be, there, in your mind. Just as you do not obsess about the constant activity of your heart, do not obsess about the constant activity of your mind. Thoughts are thoughts that float around in your head -- just let them float.

Second point:

Thoughts Can Be Distorted, Erroneous, And Unhealthy

Just because you have a thought does not mean there is any validity to the thought. Just because I think it will be too painful to risk rejection by expressing my opinion to someone does not mean that it is true. For one thing, my action might not lead to a negative reaction from the other person. Even if the person does react in a negative, critical fashion, it does not mean that I have to interpret that as rejection. Even if it is a form of rejection, it does not mean that I have to interpret it as painful. It is very positive to look at such an event in this very realistic, practical fashion. For example, rejection just makes it clear where everyone stands. In that sense, rejection is not something to be feared, but something to be accepted as new information.

Here is a common thought by individuals with chronic anxiety:

- What if I have a panic attack in front of others? It would be awful. I would be embarrassed. Reality based thinking will help us look more realistically at these types of thoughts.

- "What if I have a panic attack in front of others?" Then it will be like any other panic attack and you will need to apply what you have learned about the physiology of anxiety, return to realistic self-talk about it being a panic attack that will soon pass, and implement your breathing when it calms enough to do so.

- "It would be awful." It might be uncomfortable, but it will not be the end of the world. You may not like that possibility but you're going to go on living your life which means you may have a panic attack in public. I know you can handle it.

- "I would be embarrassed." If you interpret your panic attack as inferiority, yes, you could feel embarrassed or ashamed. But, if you realistically recognize that a panic attack is disordered anxiety and you are learning to deal with it, then it is another learning experience to demonstrate you can make progress. The willingness to face life, even if a panic attack occurs, is something you can be proud of.

It is unhealthy to worry about what someone else will think if you have a panic attack. It is healthy to accept yourself and focus on your goals, your life, your wishes, and your efforts.

How to use this information: focus on reality-based thoughts.

Again, thoughts are thoughts. We are always going to have a mind full of thoughts. It is useful to examine our thoughts and focus on realistic, healthy ones. We may not be able to change all of our negative thoughts, but we also don't have to let them run the show. We can direct our thoughts to positive, realistic, and healthy, which helps us cope.

One other point to be clear about: I'm not suggesting that you think only positive thoughts in some made-up sense of avoiding reality. Reality-based thinking helps us to be more positive and optimistic because it helps us to see real options and possibilities. Trying to have some naive positivity that white-washes reality only puts off the rude awakening when we are forced to face reality. We should never lose sight that thoughts are thoughts; they are not real. However, we can use real experiences in life to foster positive, healthy thoughts which can strengthen and encourage us.

This area, recognizing thoughts and the influence of the thoughts on our functioning, is often best aided with psychotherapy. When working with a therapist, we may be able to recognize the presence of negative, unrealistic thoughts which are fertilizing anxious feelings. A good therapist listens and provides reflection and insight in such a fashion so as to help us hear ourselves in ways we never have before. You may find that you need to take the step of psychotherapy to further your work in managing your anxiety.

Chapter 6:
How to Manage Your Activities to Reduce Anxiety

T he eighth-century Indian Buddhist scholar Shantideva said, "If you can solve your problem, then what is the need of worrying: If you can't solve your problem, what is the use of worrying."

The goal of cognitive behavioral therapy is not to tell yourself that everything is ok and there are no problems. There are, for all of us. Rather, the aim is to achieve a balanced, realistic view of different situations that allows us to react effectively and without excessive fear, anxiety, or low mood. While thought and belief challenging are useful when thoughts and beliefs are not true or when a situation is unchangeable, problem solving is good when a situation is changeable but may be fraught with anxiety.

Problems may also be connected with depression, medical issues, addiction, or family concerns. Some types can be addressed with this model include improving communication with your spouse, reducing debt, dealing with a restriction imposed by illness, adhering to new diet, quitting smoking, getting to work on time, figuring out child care, or reducing the severity of disease symptoms.

This approach is not appropriate for all problems. If you are suffering from severe depression, problems that are mostly emotional, or a serious mental illness, this approach is not adequate. In some cases, there isn't a solution in the sense that the problem will go away. The solution may be finding healthy coping mechanisms to be able to live with it. This is called emotion-focused coping and can help increase feelings of control and hopefulness and decrease stress. If this is the case, it may be more helpful to pursue a different method than problem solving.

The problem-solving approach taught with CBT has seven steps.

- Step 1: Identify and describe the problem. The first step is describing the problem in detail. Write down what it is, the time frame, who it involves, where it happens, and so on. If you think your description might be exaggerated, you can use some of the evidence-for-or-against techniques to assess it more accurately. Choose a specific problem that is likely to have a concrete solution.

- Step 2: Identify possible solutions. Brainstorm all possible solutions you can think of. Don't worry about the details at first since even a ridiculous-sounding solution can lead you to a more realistic one. Think about the advice you might give a friend in this situation or what you've done in similar situations. You can also ask others for advice. Keep an open mind.

- Step 3: Evaluate possible solutions. Once you have a few possible solutions, write down the pros and cons of each one. In some cases, you may need professional advice from a doctor, lawyer, or administrator.

- Step 4: Decide on optimal and backup solutions. Based on the pros and cons of the possible solutions, decide on the best solution and one or two backup solutions. Alternatively, you can simply rank the solutions in order of preference.

- Step 5: Plan what you need to do. Plan out detailed steps needed to enact the solution you identified. Breaking it down into small steps can make it more approachable.

- Step 6: Carry out your plan. Do the steps you listed in Step 5. If needed, shift to one of your backup plans.

- Step 7: Study and adjust plan as needed. How did it go? Is the problem solved or reduced to a manageable level? If the problem is not solved or if a new problem has arisen, you can return to Step 1 and formulate a new solution and plan. See the workbook in the appendix for a guide.

Sleep

There are things you can do in your life outside the CBT strategies that can greatly benefit your well-being and increase the effectiveness of any therapy you use. One of the most important factors is sleep. Getting enough sleep is important for mood, energy levels, physical health, and even the chemical balance of the brain. Things like anxiety can make it harder to sleep, creating a reinforcing cycle of stress and exhaustion. However, there are many simple changes you can make to help yourself get a good night's sleep:

- Try to sleep and get up at the same time every day and to sleep when you feel tired.

- Don't oversleep by more than an hour to make up for lost sleep.

- Don't watch TV, use electronics, or eat in bed.

- Give yourself thirty minutes to an hour before bed to relax.

- Avoid napping more than twenty minutes during the day if it makes it hard to sleep at night.

- Not everyone needs eight hours of sleep per night. Focus on getting restful sleep, rather than getting "enough" sleep, which can lead to more anxiety.

- Make sure that your bedroom is quiet, dark, comfortable, and free from distractions.

- Avoid caffeine, alcohol, and nicotine in the four hours before going to bed, or avoid them entirely if you find that you are sensitive to their effects.

- Get physical activity during the day, but not late in the evening.

- Ask your doctor about the side effects of medications—some can lead to trouble sleeping.

Healthy Eating

Many people also find that a healthier diet contributes to a better sense of overall well-being. It can also contribute to weight loss and improvement of other health factors, relieving anxiety in the process. If you feel that addressing your diet now would lead to more anxiety, leave it for a later time. However, if you feel motivated to improve your diet, go for it. It could be an effective way to feel healthier and less anxious or depressed.

The Mediterranean and DASH (Dietary Approaches to Stop Hypertension) diets are some of the best supported in terms of scientific literature, and both can be delicious, flexible, and sustainable in the long term. Outside specific approaches, you can simply aim to eat more fruits, vegetables, whole grains, fish, healthy fats like olive oil and avocado, nuts and seeds, while opting for less red meat, high-fat dairy, white flour and refined grains, sugars, hydrogenated oils, and processed foods. If you enjoy cooking, taking cooking classes and making healthier home-cooked meals could be a great part of your behavioral-activation strategy.

Physical Activity

Physical activity is a way to improve mood. Physical activity does not have to mean exercise. Many people believe that they must go to the gym and run on a treadmill or ride a stationary bike for it to count. This is not at all true! There are many enjoyable ways to be active that don't take you anywhere near a gym. Walking, biking, and hiking outside can be fun and relaxing, and research shows that a brisk walk can be just as helpful as a run for improving long-term health. Winter sports like skiing and skating are great too. Low-intensity activities like gardening, playing catch with your child, doing yard work, or actively cleaning the house count as well.

Mantra Meditation

Meditation is a great way to relieve stress and cultivate mindfulness. There are many approaches, but one easy way to begin is mantra meditation. It is a form of meditation in which one chooses a sound or phrase and repeats it anywhere from a few to hundreds of times. It can be as simple as a soothing sound, such as "om" or "ahh," or it can be a phrase in any language expressing sentiments of compassion, kindness, or peace. You can make one up yourself or use a traditional ancient mantra that has been murmured for centuries. There is really great flexibility in mantra meditation, making this powerful technique all the more approachable.

Choosing a Mantra

Simple mantras can be soothing and help you clear your mind during meditation, and compassionate phrases can give you a chance to fully absorb the message. We will suggest several traditional mantras to get you started, and then provide suggestions for how to create your own.

The most well-known mantra is also the simplest: om. Hindu, Jain, and other traditions teach that it is the original sound of the universe and that it has a deep spiritual power signifying the three characteristics of divine energy: creation, preservation, and liberation. Regardless of the beliefs associated with it, the om mantra has uniquely soothing qualities. The sounds feel natural and produce a calming vibration that supports both mental and physical relaxation.

When chanting the om mantra, you'll really be making three sounds. Begin with an "ah" sound then let it shift into an "oo." At the end, close your lips to make the humming "mmm" sound. This last one should resonate throughout your chest. You can hold each sound for as long as you like and then pause briefly before repeating. You can expand on the om mantra by chanting "om shanti, shanti, shanti," which means "om peace, peace, peace."

Another simple mantra is Sat nam, which translates to "Truth is my name." The "saaat" portion is pronounced for eight to thirty-five times as long as the "nam" portion, resulting in a resonance in the chest that, much like om, is calming.

A slightly longer option with the same sort of calming effect is Ra ma da sa, sa say so hung. It means "Sun, moon, earth, infinity—all that is in infinity, I am thee." Traditionally, this mantra is accompanied by a specific pose. Sit comfortably and press your upper arms against your sides. Bend your elbows at a ninety-degree angle, and turn your palms to face upward. Kundalini yoga practitioners believe that this mantra and pose are restorative and send healing energy to the self and others.

A good option for a simple, traditional compassionate mantra is Lokah samastah sukhino bhavantu. It is pronounced "low-kah sa-ma-stah soo-ki-no ba-van-too" and roughly translates to "May all beings everywhere be happy and free." A quick Internet search will turn up dozens of videos offering help with pronunciation or simply repeating the mantra multiple times as a meditation aid.

A slightly longer mantra expressing good wishes toward other is as follows:

Sarvesham svastir bhavatu (ser-vay-sham sva-steer ba-va-too)

Sarvesham shantir bhavatu (ser-vay-sham shan-teer ba-va-too)

Sarvesham purnam bhavatu (ser-vay-sham puur-nam ba-va-too)

Sarvesham mangalam bhavatu (ser-vay-sham mang-ga-lam ba-va-too)

It expresses a wish for well-being for all, peace for all, wholeness for all, and happiness for all. Again, you can find many videos online that can help you get the hang of chanting by searching for this phrase.

If none of these mantras resonate with you, or if you'd just like to make something more personal, you can create your own mantra. It can be as simple as a sound—play around with making different "ahh," "eee," and "hmmm" sounds until you find one that feels soothing and calming. To create a compassionate mantra, first think of the sentiment you want to express. It could be related to loving-kindness and acceptance toward yourself and others, wishes for peace, or anything else you want to remind yourself of. Then, try to find words that fit the meaning and that are easy and pleasant to say many times in a row. Work on paper if you find it helpful or simply say the words aloud. Things like "love for all beings" or "peace within and without" could work. Once you've chosen a mantra, you can begin the meditation!

Beginning Mantra Meditation

First, choose a quiet, comfortable place where you won't be interrupted. Sit on a couch, comfortable chair, or yoga mat, lie on your bed, or lean against a pillow. If you're sitting on the ground, you can make it more comfortable by sitting on a small pillow or folded blanket so that you can keep your back straight and let your knees fall gently outward. Place your hands on your thighs, or press them lightly together in front of you. Avoid bright lights, as they can be overly stimulating.

Focus on your breathing. Breathe in a deep and relaxed manner, but don't try to control the breath. Breathe naturally. Start by focusing on your intention. It could be something like deepening self-compassion, increasing kindness to others, or letting go. Many people find that choosing an intention for their meditation session helps them stay focused and brings it deeper meaning.

Begin chanting your sound or phrase. If you have chosen a traditional Sanskrit mantra, you can find guides online to help with pronunciation, but this isn't the most important thing. Simply chant with a tone and speed that feels comfortable.

Draw your attention to the vibrations created by the mantra. This will be particularly noticeable with the om mantra, which you should be able to feel throughout your chest and belly. If thoughts come to your mind, gently let them go. It is normal to feel distracted or frustrated during meditation sometimes. There is no perfection to be achieved— it is enough to simply try. Repeat the chant for a few minutes. You can continue chanting for as long as you wish, or shift to silent meditation.

For those who follow a faith, repetitive contemplation of any prayer or passage from scripture can be effective as well. Choose any passage from your holy book and chant it again and again silently, all the while paying attention to the words. Enjoy each word and every phrase. Listen to yourself as you recite the passage. What insights and reflections does it awaken in you? Watch your response to this prayer. And when you finish, spend a few seconds by yourself in divine silence.

To get the full benefits of meditation, it's recommended to do it every day. Try to set aside ten to fifteen minutes each day to do mantra meditation of another kind.

Chapter 7:
Ways to Find Instant Calm and Overcome Anxiety

When I first started talking therapy, I really struggled to connect in the sessions. At the start, whenever the therapist asked me questions about my trauma or the things that had happened in my life to make me disassociate, it was easy to talk. It was like I was explaining someone else's situation rather than my own. But then, I would have trouble remembering what we had talked about. Other times, I couldn't speak at all. It was so frustrating; I just wanted to make progress and not feel like I was wasting my therapist's time.

The skills below worked well for me when I have been in triggering situations and I've needed to reconnect. All your feelings are normal and a high percentage of people in a similar position have similar experiences. There isn't a right or wrong way to feel.

1. Try and notice objects around you. What color are they? What shape is the object? Are there any details on it? This will start to bring your awareness back into the space that you are in.

2. How do you feel? Are you hot or cold? Are you hungry or thirsty?

3. What can you hear? Can you hear cars, or birds or even a ticking clock?

4. Try wiggling your fingers and toes. Next, move your head from side to side. Can you feel the ground? Notice the pressure under your feet or the chair you're sat in.

Now that you're becoming aware, know that you are in control. You may need to practice these steps 5 or 6 times while you are present in the moment to recall them when you need them. Having them stuck on a bathroom mirror or on the inside of a kitchen cupboard will help you to remember the steps too.

5. Keep something small in a coat or trouser pocket, or an easy access pocket in your bag. When you feel yourself disconnecting, reach for it and hold it in your hand. Notice its texture. Is it smooth or rough? Play with it or squeeze it.

I always have a crystal in my coat pocket, just in case. I have a variety of different shapes; some polished, others not. They can be something special or pebbles from the garden. A friend of mine uses an old farthing.

Don't forget to breathe slowly and deeply. To make it more powerful, link it with looking into a mirror into your own eyes. I've done this in a coffee shop bathroom and when I've been on a train. I've even used the camera on my phone, just remember to flip the or the camera around so you can see yourself. The more you practice the more you'll become a pro!

If you feel your heart is racing and feel like your panicking, try slowing down your breathing. After therapy sessions, I was left feeling disconnected from myself and the world around me. I felt as if I was in a bubble. My therapy sessions were held in the town center and I could easily feel confused and scared. I would walk endlessly around, not knowing what I was doing. I will not leave you feeling that way. Box breathing is an amazing skill to have and will help you in any situation, either to prepare you for tough times ahead or to help you take stock afterwards.

How to Box Breathe

1. Start with sitting or lying down, whichever is the most comfortable for you

2. Take a slow deep breath in for a count of 4

3. Hold that breath for 4 counts

4. Now breath out for a count of 4

5. Wait for 4 counts before repeating steps 2–5

Do this at least 5 times, longer if needed. If, after doing this, you're feeling low, put on your favorite music. Anything that makes you want to sing and dance is the fastest way to shift your emotions.

Be proud of your achievements. Even if it takes you multiple times to grasp the breathing exercise, just practicing the steps will have a positive impact on your life, even if you don't feel it working straight away. The more you do it, the deeper it's going into your mind.

Now it's time to be kind to yourself and celebrate what you have just done. Do something that makes you feel loved and recharges your soul. It could be spending time with your pet or being present with your kids. Personally, I reward myself with a treat night and a movie that'll make me laugh, or spending time with someone that I love. Try not to reward yourself with treats that could have a negative response later on, such as alcohol or drugs.

The breathing skill can be used in some extremely volatile and highly stressful situations to calm and control your flight or fight mode.

If you've ever wondered how a firefighter has the courage to go into a burning building, you can bet they've used box breathing to control their fears and overcome their bodies natural responses so that they are in full control. They're trained for these situations, but if they let their emotions take over, all that training is out the window as their bodies go into the primal mode of fight or flight. Our bodies react to what's going on in the mind, whether it's a real threat to your life or it's all in your head. The brain can't tell the difference. So it does what it needs to protect us.

Before I learned how to control my anxiety through breathing, I was taking large doses of beta blockers just to be able to leave my apartment to take the rubbish to the bins. In fact, my panic attacks were so bad that I didn't leave home for over a year. Learning to box breathe allowed me to feel in control in the small situations that would normally cause me to panic. Being able to go for a coffee with a friend, for instance. Don't get me wrong, I still had my moments, but they were few and far between now. After a good 3 months, I was able to come off all my anxiety medication, with supervision from my doctor, and I could return to work.

Speak to your doctor before changing anything. They may be able to give you a support network or suggest alternatives for you. For me, I needed to come off beta blockers, antidepressants and sleeping pills for my own sanity. They just left me feeling like I didn't know what day it was, or which way was up or down!

Chapter 8:

Getting in Tune with Your Thoughts and Feelings

You may be thinking 'What does this have to do with my anxiety issues?' Well, trust me, it has everything to do with resolving anxiety! Emotional awareness is all about being able to recognize and understand your emotions and how they affect or influence your behavior.

We have already seen how anxiety issues or occurrence of a situation that triggers your anxiety issues and fear can trigger a relapse and the various ways in which you can avoid that from happening. However, during the process, there are so many emotional changes that take place, and if you are going to respond well to situations, you have to be aware of your emotions.

The good thing is that you know how you feel and the reasons why you feel that way. This simply means that you can see how your emotions can be helpful or hurtful to what you do. In such a situation, there is also a chance that you are aware of how people view you. But there is a huge difference between emotional intelligence and cognitive self-awareness, which mainly pays attention to your thoughts and ideas instead of your feelings.

Emotional intelligence is one of the core competencies that help you manage your emotions, relationships, and awareness of others. Here are various steps that you can follow to help you develop awareness of your feelings and how they are interconnected with your thoughts.

Step 1: Choose A Triggering Situation

By now, you already know the things that trigger anger, anxiety and upsetting feelings for you. Try to put them down on paper and select one that is least challenging to you just for starters. The reason why we begin with the least challenging is so you can practice your skills successfully one at a time until you can face your worst fears.

This may take days to weeks, hence the need for patience. Try to stretch yourself out of your comfort zone while still ensuring that you do not get overwhelmed in the process. However, if you feel that this process is emotionally overwhelming, it is important that you seek help from someone that can work with you like a therapist, friend or family member.

Step 2: Center Yourself in the Present While Taking in Slow And Deep Breaths

Once you know what trigger you would like to work on, it is important that you pause for a moment and close your eyes. Take in slow and deep breaths for about 5-10 minutes. Breath from your belly and allow your whole body to come to the point of relaxation.

Focus your mind on your breath with your eyes closed. In your mind, scan your body from head to toe allowing every tension to be released. Let loose every tightness in your body so that you relax.

Now, start imagining yourself at a safe place. Try to remind yourself that you are not the emotions or the thoughts but just an observer and a person that can choose the thoughts and emotions that appeal to you. How does that make you feel? Do you feel that you are in charge of your body, responses, thoughts, and feelings? Imagine not having anyone around you making you feel what you do not want to without your permission. You are simply the observer of your emotional feelings.

Now, start shifting your mind into creating a mental note to yourself. In this note, tell yourself that the emotions you are experiencing are old energy pockets, wounds that come from your past experiences, and your childhood. Tell yourself that this is okay because during that time, you had no cognitive ability to know or even see yourself from different points of view. Now, you have become an intelligent adult who is well able to take charge of all processes and changes taking place in your life.

Repeat it over and over until your brain gets a positive attitude towards your inner and outer person.

If you need to stop this exercise in the middle of it at any time, you can do so if necessary, otherwise, ensure that you can do it to the end without any interruptions.

Step 3: Identify And Feel Your Emotions

While feeling centered in your breathing, start to bring that trigger into your mind. You can do this by simply trying to recall the latest/most recent occurrence. Avoid making any judgments and pause for a moment to get in touch with your feelings and sensations. Take note of any emotions and feelings you had inside.

Now, try to take deep and slow breaths while still feeling what you felt when you had the occurrence. Begin to ask yourself what you are feeling at that moment. Do you feel anger? Do you feel scared? Are you anxious? Start looking for the emotions that run beneath it. Anger is but a secondary emotion that comes on as a means of trying to protect yourself from feeling vulnerable.

Is there something that underlies that anger? Is it hurt, shame, fear or something else? What emotional feelings do you have? Write them down on a plain sheet of paper or in a journal.

Step 4: Feel and Take Note of The Location of Sensations in Your Body

At this point, it is critical that you take a moment, pause and feel each emotion run through your body. Take note of the sensations that you feel at different parts of your body. For each of the emotions that is triggered, record the sensation you feel and what part of the body you feel it in. You can do this by ensuring that you maintain the picture of your triggering event in your mind.

while you're at it, take in deep breaths and place your hand(s) on the place where you feel the sensation. As you do this, begin to let go of any impulse that pulls you towards judging, stopping, repressing or fixing your emotions and sensations. Keep probing your emotions and taking note of the emotional feelings until they lessen in intensity.

If you feel that anger is primary, keep asking yourself whether there is something other than anger that you are feeling. Give a description of your sensations and the body parts where you feel them. Record them and keep repeating this until you have exhausted all the primary emotions.

Step 5: Accept Your Feelings And Have The Confidence That You Can Handle Your Emotions And Sensations

Here, it is important that you keep reminding yourself that your emotions do not define who you are. You are not your emotions but just an observer of your emotions. Tell yourself that those emotions that you have are energy, and your feelings are pockets or charged energy that is associated directly with your past pains and wounds.

In other words, as a choice maker for your life, you have the free will to choose what you want. You can breathe into painful, fearful and anxious situations. As you do that, notice those sensations, and emotional feelings shift, move away and allow yourself to release them. Affirm to yourself that you have the power to accept these feelings as they are at that very moment.

Start telling yourself that you can handle it. Tell yourself that you are strong enough to handle the situation with ease, calm and wisdom. Realize that one of the most powerful leverages that you have over negative emotions is reminding yourself about the time you had them and how you handled them successfully.

In other words, if you have been able to handle this well in the past, there is a strong possibility that you can handle it again in the present and future. Tell yourself that you have done so in the past and you can do it again and again in the future. Keep repeating the affirmations as many times as you possibly can or until you experience a smooth shift of emotional state and intensity.

Allow yourself to take in slow and deep breaths throughout the body and in between the repetitions. Bear in mind that every time you handle the emotion, you add that into your repertoire of success. This will eventually grow and strengthen your confidence as well as your ability to handle similar situations in the future. This will allow you to pick up lessons that will help you turn fear-based emotions into assets.

Step 6: Identify What You Tell Yourself in Your Mind That Triggers Pain

Now, start taking note of your thoughts as you picture the triggering event. Record any toxic thoughts and feelings that come through your mind. The truth is that what you think often triggers an emotional feeling and physical sensations in your body. This is just how the brain functions.

All you have to do here is to watch those thoughts from afar. Remember that you are not the emotion or the thoughts; you are simply an observer that is taking note of things as they happen without making any judgments.

Whenever you get disturbing thoughts, imagine riding in a luxurious speeding train. Imagine that you are looking out the window, taking note of every thought or emotion that causes anger and then quickly close the window as you get back to your comfortable seat - your safe place.

Record everything that you tell yourself while you have that self-talk adjacent to the emotions and physical sensations you experienced.

Step 7: Empathetically Connect So That You Can Understand And Validate Your Experiences

It is important to keep reminding yourself that even though other people or situations may trigger a painful feeling in you, they are not the cause of your pain. It is your self-talk that is causing you so much pain. It is what you tell yourself that is triggering the resentment, anger, guilt, and frustration among other emotions you may be experiencing.

It is the thing you tell yourself that is causing the physical body sensations you have. Well, trust me, this is good news! The main reason why I say this is because the way you explain your triggers to yourself is the cause of your emotional feelings. It is what causes you to get upset.

The thing is: you can change that. The way to do this is to choose to tell yourself something positive no matter the situation. Think thoughts that cause you to be calm, empowered and loaded with confidence. This is the best way in which you can start making informed decisions and choices.

Start making a mental note telling yourself how this is really good news. In other words, you are telling yourself that you are the one in charge of what emotional response you experience, the thoughts that you have as well as the actions that you take.

Understand that your happiness is your responsibility. For you to achieve that peace of mind irrespective of what the triggering event is, it is only you that can find it. There is no other person who can make you feel a certain way when you do not want to feel that way. You only feel what you feel because you want to.

When you allow this to sink into your spirit, you will find yourself creating statements that give affirmations that simply validate your experience. Start telling yourself, 'it is okay that I feel overwhelmed' rather than telling yourself that you cannot handle it, you can never get things done, or even that it is too much for you.

That said, remember that thoughts are what trigger feelings. It is then that feelings communicate important information on how you can handle your life to thrive or survive worse situations. When you grow your awareness of the emotions and sensations you experience, you gain more understanding of the strong connection between self-talk and what you feel.

Once you do, you realize that you have so much power you never thought you had, hence you can now regulate your emotional state as you wish. You realize that when you make small changes in your thought process, you chart the course of your life by simply making a conscious choice of how you experience different events. You simply experience situations in ways that enrich the direction that you have chosen.

Your painful emotions allow you to know whether you are on the right path to emotional fulfillment or not. Once you know the power that emotions have on shaping your life and the way they work hand in hand with your thoughts, it will be much easier to stop despising them. Just remember that in this sea of life, your navigation system is what you allow yourself to feel.

Chapter 9:
The Importance of Sleep When Trying to Stop Anxiety and Worry

I am frequently surprised at how many patients' anxiety symptoms improve or resolve altogether with just a few nights of deep, restful, restorative sleep. The reason is that our mind recharges its neurochemistry hormones primarily when we are in states of relaxation or deep sleep. This means that given the proper amount of sleep, our anxious minds can often correct themselves.

Sleep and wakefulness are produced by the complex interaction of internal biological clocks, environmental influences, and activities that either stimulate arousal or induce sleep. Humans wake and sleep in twenty-four-hour cycles—usual sixteen hours of wakefulness followed by eight hours of sleep. These cycles are under the influence of the circadian pacemaker, also known as the suprachiasmatic nucleus in the brain. The suprachiasmatic nucleus is affected by several factors, including sunlight, the production of melatonin and certain neurotransmitters, and the brain receptors that provide feedback from the internal environment.

The primary element that sets our biological clocks is light. Special photoreceptors in the retina of the eye are stimulated by outdoor light levels, which reach one hundred thousand lux (a unit of light energy) as opposed to office room light at two hundred to four hundred lux. When you spend just a few minutes outdoors, your circadian clock is set. Spending the whole day in office room light levels will not set your circadian clock. It seems the worst idea of the industrial age was the invention of the lightbulb!

The special photoreceptors in the retina send signals directly to the suprachiasmatic nucleus (one on each side of the brain). The suprachiasmatic nucleus also receives wakeful signals in the morning from the adrenal glands in the form of adrenal corticoid hormones. The great mystery is what happens in the brain that permits us to fall asleep?

One component of the answer is melatonin. During the day, the suprachiasmatic nucleus inhibits melatonin production. Later in the day, melatonin production begins to ramp up due to the release of the neurotransmitter norepinephrine in the pineal gland. Melatonin quiets and suppresses the wakeful signal from the suprachiasmatic nucleus, allowing us to fall asleep. Recent research and drug development has focused on melatonin receptors in an attempt to find a safe and effective way to induce sleep.

Melatonin helps us adapt to basic environmental rhythms, such as night and day. As night falls, melatonin increases and becomes a key player in signaling the start of various mental and physical restorative processes. It also accounts for much of the body's temperature rhythm, allowing the nighttime temperature drop required for sleep. Unlike serotonin, melatonin passes through the blood-brain barrier and can therefore be taken as a supplement.

Most of the brain's melatonin is generated in the pineal gland through the conversion of serotonin. The pineal gland has a particularly elaborate blood-vessel system and serves as a key modulator of the entire neurohormonal system. It is the gearshift that allows us to adapt to changing environmental conditions. Because the pineal gland is light sensitive due to connections with the optic nerves, it allows the brain to perceive the time of day.

Like serotonin, melatonin helps the nervous system adapt to a changing environment with the least amount of stress. Melatonin and serotonin inhibit the sympathetic nervous system (fight-or-flight response) and stimulate the parasympathetic system, which is associated with calming. Melatonin increases GABA, another important neurochemical in mood regulation.

Like serotonin, melatonin affects prostaglandins, which seem to play a critical role in depression. A melatonin deficiency has been linked to depressed mood, sleep disruption, disturbed body rhythms, agitation, and higher body temperature. Melatonin levels have been found to be high during the manic phase of bipolar illness and low during the depressive phase.

Like with serotonin, melatonin levels are low with premenstrual syndrome. Alcoholics (even if recovered) have lower melatonin levels. In seasonal affective disorder, too much melatonin is released during the day with a drop-off at night. Light therapy suppresses daytime melatonin, allowing for a nighttime surge, which is the normal fluctuation of the circadian rhythm.

Treating sleep disturbances with melatonin is well established. One-half to ten milligrams may be needed to affect the brain's clock. It should be taken near bedtime, unless you are trying to reset your clock (e.g., taking the dose several hours before bedtime if traveling east against time zones or in the morning if traveling west).

Another recent drug development focuses on facilitating the brain's ability to shift gears from the wakefulness circuit of neurochemicals to the sleep circuit. A new sleep medication, Elsmore, is a highly selective antagonist for brain orexin receptors OX1R and OX2R. The mechanism by which Belsomra counteracts insomnia is through blocking orexin receptors. The orexin neuropeptide signaling system is a central promoter of wakefulness, so Belsomra shuts off the wakefulness circuit so the sleep circuit can take over. This transfer of activation from one circuit to another takes all of five seconds when it occurs. Belsomra is non-habit forming and takes several days to reach maximum benefit. It should be taken thirty minutes before your desired bedtime.

The level of our relaxation, restfulness, and sleep can be determined by examining brain-wave patterns on an electroencephalogram (EEG) machine. During wakefulness when focus and concentration are required, our brain waves are in a beta pattern, which is short and stimulating. While daydreaming, we fall into an alpha pattern, which is also true when we are meditating or in REM sleep (known as rapid eye movement sleep, light sleep when most dreams occur).

Delta and theta patterns are seen at the deeper, restorative levels of sleep and in certain deep meditation, or in trancelike states experienced in a flotation sensory-deprivation tank. These patterns are necessary for feeling well rested. In fact, you should go into these levels of deeper sleep two to three times a night for up to an hour each time.

This school-book account of the biophysiology of sleep is not itself meant to be a sleep aid, but it's just to point out how complex and multifactorial the processes of sleep and wakefulness are. If we don't respect this and acknowledge our physical limitations and needs, we are doomed to take a pill for every bodily function. I have patients who need to take a pill to go to sleep, then one to wake up, then one to calm down, and one to stay alert. They need one to have a bowel movement, one to allow their urine to flow comfortably, and one to calm their stomachs so they can eat. Then they need one to have an erection because they are too tired and not in balance.

The causes of insomnia are many. About 90 percent of those with anxiety or depression report difficulty sleeping. Conversely, insomnia is also thought to be a possible cause of depression, not just a symptom. Many medical problems can be contributing factors to insomnia, such as chronic pain, osteoarthritis, gastroesophageal reflux disease, asthma, emphysema, snoring with sleep apnea, alcoholism, and restless leg syndrome.

Several prescription and over-the-counter medications and supplements have a stimulatory effect that could result in sleep disturbance. In addition, more than seven million Americans regularly work at night or have a rotating shift schedule. Constant changes in the time you go to bed, eat meals, and do certain activities can produce disruption in natural circadian rhythms, which leads to insomnia.

Healthy Sleep Hygiene

Before considering a medical treatment or over-the-counter remedy for insomnia, you should first look at your sleep hygiene practices. Recent studies show that meditation and behavioral-therapy techniques are more effective at restoring normal sleep architecture than any medication! Basic guidelines for overcoming insomnia and achieving restful, healthy sleep include the following:

- Keep a regular schedule of when you go to bed and when you get up.

- Avoid afternoon naps that keep you from falling asleep at night.

- Do your exercise in the morning, not late in the day.

- Avoid alcohol and caffeine within six hours of bedtime.

- Use the bedroom for sleep and sex. Don't read, watch TV, do paperwork, answer the phone, have arguments, or do anything stressful in the sleep environment.

- Make sure the bedroom is quiet, dark, and comfortable. If you live in a noisy area, buy a device to create white noise, such as a fan, or use earplugs, if needed. Get blackout drapes for the window if too much light is shining through.

- Go to bed in a relaxed mood. If you're not relaxed, consider eating a snack high in carbohydrates, such as grains, legumes, pasta, bread, vegetables, fruits, or cereal.

- Don't lie in bed awake, thinking and worrying. Get up and leave the bedroom, go to the bathroom, eat a snack, or watch part of the late-night movie. When you feel sleepy and relaxed, go back to the bedroom.

Herbal Sedatives

Often, a sedative is helpful to induce sleep and restore normal sleep architecture, especially in those whose sleep patterns have been disrupted by illness, international travel, or anxiety. You should be following all the above advice on proper sleep hygiene before turning to a supplement or medication. You should also not mix alcohol or drugs with any sleep remedy. Those with addictive personalities should stay away from sedative medications unless prescribed by a physician who knows you well.

For centuries, man has used herbal remedies to promote sleep. Unfortunately, there are only a few placebo-controlled studies to demonstrate their efficacy. The neuro-pharmacologic properties of these compounds are not always known, and their mechanism of action, active ingredients, and effective dose are sometimes uncertain. These remedies include the following:

- Kava kava: Although helpful for anxiety and insomnia, this herb has been associated with liver toxicity and withdrawal side effects. It should not be mixed with alcohol or sedative drugs or taken more than twenty-five weeks straight.

- Valerian root: From the plant Valeriana officinalis, this herb has shown benefit in the treatment of insomnia in some studies. It has been used for thousands of years in India and China as a sleep enhancer.

- Chamomile: This herb is widely used in the Western world as a treatment for anxiety, nervous stomach, and relaxation. It can be found in small amounts in a tea form or more effectively dosed through a standardized extract. The active ingredient, apigenin, works on GABA receptors much like the benzodiazepine medications.

- Hops: Humulus lupulus, the hops plant, has scaly, cone-like fruits known to have medicinal properties. Besides their use in flavoring and preserving beer, they contain a chemical (dimethylvinyl) that causes the tranquilizing effects of this plant. It is available as an extract or essential oil.

- Passion flower: Passiflora incarnate, or the passion flower, is native to North America and is used for nervousness, restlessness, anxiety, insomnia, and irritability. As a sleeping aid, it is known for having no hangover sedation in the morning.

- California poppy: This flower (eschscholtzia californica) is gaining in popularity as a sleep aid and stress reducer. The active ingredients are alkaloids, just like the opium poppy, but without the addictive properties.

- Lavender aromatherapy: Insomniacs have been shown to sleep better if their rooms are scented with lavender. A hot lavender bath, in which several drops of the oil are placed in a tub full of comfortably hot water, may be better than a sedative for calming your nerves, relaxing your muscles, and preparing your mind for rest.

Homeopathic and Over-the-Counter Sleep Remedies

Homeopathic remedies include the following:

- Ignatia is used for worry, insomnia, anxiety, and emotional stress.

- Pulsatilla is used for insomnia and anxiety.

- Sleep Ease, made by Lehning Laboratories in France, is a nonaddictive sleep aid first available in Europe and now being distributed in the United States.

- Natural Calm is a magnesium supplement made by Natural Vitality in ionic form to increase bioavailability. Magnesium relaxes the muscles and reduces anxiety, headaches, irritability, and heart irregularities. Take at bedside to see if you naturally fall and stay asleep better.

- Kavinace Ultra PM is 650 mg of a proprietary blend with 3 mg of melatonin that is made by NeuroScience. It claims to act by helping the brain maintain good levels of calming neurotransmitters, such as GABA, melatonin, and serotonin. I have had patients recommend this, so that's how I know about it.

- 5-HTP is created in the body from the amino acid tryptophan. It is then used in the synthesis of serotonin, the brain neurotransmitter most responsible for healthy sleep cycles. Because 5-HTP crosses easily into the brain across the blood-brain barrier, it ultimately causes an increase in the brain's serotonin levels. The supplement is considered safe and is generally well tolerated.

- Melatonin is marketed as a dietary supplement that has been shown to improve sleep. It is available in a number of forms (tablets, time-release capsules, under-the-tongue lozenges, liquid extract, and tea). Of course, you should cooperate with the melatonin in trying to regulate your circadian rhythms by going to bed at a regular time and following the other sleep hygiene recommendations. Doses of three to six milligrams thirty minutes before bedtime are most common, but I have seen patients who need up to fifteen milligrams to get the benefit.

Two over-the-counter antihistamines that do not require a prescription have been approved by the FDA for use as sleeping aids. They are diphenhydramine and doxylamine. These are the drugs most commonly found in "PM" products, such as Tylenol PM, Unisom, and Sominex. Although the drugs are available over the counter and are generally safe and nonaddictive, it is illegal to drive a motor vehicle while under the influence of these drugs if you are drowsy and impaired by them!

Chapter 10:
Changing Your Lifestyle to Regain Control of Your Life

We all have worries in our hearts and minds. We worry about putting on too much weight, how much money we have, the snowball of bills that come into our mailbox each month, and all the other things that affect our lives routinely. Although this is a normal thing for most people, some people struggle with depression and anxiety as a result of life's worries. Their concerns severely affect their ability to function properly and do normal things in everyday life. This is a stumbling block to helping people get on the road to where they want to be. We are now going to talk about how to deal with life's worries and anxiety and act appropriately.

Fight or Flight

When it comes to dealing with life's problems, different people act in different ways by facing a problem or by fleeing the scene. Many people are tempted to run away from scenarios that could get them into trouble and put them into an unfortunate situation. If you can avoid such a situation, you can also flee from the stress of that situation. Even so, it is not possible to avoid such situations all the time. Sometimes you have to face the problems of your life, as Maria said in The Sound of Music. It is, therefore, best to figure out ways that you can respond to the things that are stressing you out.

To combat stress is to exercise. Then you can fight the worries that are clouding your mind. Exercise is one way to get rid of stress by releasing endorphins. You can feel good after one workout, which will help improve your mood and relieve you from the burdensome cares of life. Exercise will also help you feel less nervous.

The fight-or-flight response is our body's natural instinct that we can use for our benefit. It is our coping mechanism when faced with situations that are naturally difficult. Our fight-or-flight response can help us to escape situations that could be dangerous. For example, when a fierce animal is coming toward us, we respond by running away from the place. It is important to bear in mind that it can help us or hinder us from moving forward with our lives and the most important thing is to learn how to face our problems.

Structured Problem-Solving

Before you deal with a problem, it is crucial that you first think of the best way to respond to the situation. When you do a simulation, you will know how you should deal with a particular situation. This will help you solve the problem. If you usually worry a lot, you will find that you will feel better after confronting your problems proactively with an understanding of the issue. There will be no surprises this way and you will be able to handle the situation in a positive way. Solving problems is going to help you experience greater happiness. When you know how to handle all the challenges that life throws your way, you will feel better and more confident.

Limit Your Consumption of Media

Technology is beneficial for us, but it can also prove to be harmful. There's no doubt that social media can be a source of stress in our lives. We compulsively check Facebook or Instagram for the latest notifications, and then we see messages that make us worry. However, if you intentionally limit your screen time and your interactions on social media, you will find that it is liberating, and you will be free of the chains that bind you to your online profile. In addition, you will experience fewer things that distract you. This will give you more productivity in your life. Try to spend a month without the distraction of social media. Get away from it for a little while and see the difference in your overall morale. You will feel much better.

Too many of us spend over four or five hours on our phones every day. We answer messages, spend time on Facebook, surf the Web, watch movies, and do other things. Consuming more media is going to lead to more stress, and therefore, we should be mindful to avoid it as much as possible. Limit your screen time to only a few hours a day; you will feel better. Read a book. Go outside and enjoy the sunshine. Take a walk.

Try Meditation or Aromatherapy

When you feel tired by the weight of everyday stresses, you might feel that there is no way to get out of it. However, you should simply find a place where you can be quiet and relaxed with some soothing music that will calm your mind. Find a place where you can allow the stress to pass away. Furthermore, you can enhance this experience by including some aromatherapy. So, get some candles and scented oils that will put you in your happy place and calm your spirits. You will feel like the clouds have lifted from your mind and that the sun has come out and is shining over your heart and mind. It's a new day. Enjoy it! You deserve to be happy. Be good to yourself.

Take a Shower or Hot Bath

Another method that will help you feel loads better is if you jump into the shower or take a hot bath. You will feel that your muscles relax, and your whole body will feel a lot better. So, go right ahead. Get into the water. Experience the joy of the stress being rinsed away with the water that is flowing gently against your skin. You can also try aquatic therapy. Visit your local pool and allow yourself to swim the stress away. You will feel the difference, not only in your physical body but also in your mind. It is a full body experience that you will not regret doing.

Rest and Experience Freedom like No Other

One of the things we tend to neglect in our lives is getting enough rest. We power through the day and go on with our limitless supply of caffeine in our coffee and other energy drinks. We find ourselves spending more time on the computer. And often, we answer work-related inquiries well into the night while getting five or six hours of sleep. We just don't know how to take a load off and get away from work. That is especially the case with people who live in the United States who are prone to workaholism. We work more than ever before. We put on more weight than before and live an unhealthy lifestyle. We need to learn to do how to rest and get more of it. It is vital that we rest and relax from all the cares of this life. Think about ways that you can do this.

- Sleep like a baby at night

Sleep is one of the most neglected things when life gets busy. However, we should remember that if we get more sleep, we feel healthier and happier. Getting enough rest at night is one of the ways to improve our quality of life. We can feel a lot better if we just get the right amount of shut-eye, and that usually amounts to eight to nine hours of sleep a night. You may be thinking, "Am I going to be able to do that with my busy schedule, three kids to take care of, wife to love, etc.?"

Well, you should make sleep an important part of your wellness routine. Aside from giving you the physical benefit of feeling at your best, sleep gives us a mood boost, and we don't need to rely on as much caffeine in our system. Instead, we feel like we have more energy, and then we can go about our day with feelings of happiness. Try to get more sleep and you will feel the significant change it brings to your overall health. Plus, you'll protect your body against diseases and illnesses that can easily bring you down. Sleep more for your health.

- Go right ahead and take that nap

Napping also has proven health benefits. Even a short twenty-minute nap can boost your mood and give you the needed energy to keep going through your day. Sometimes, naps can help you recover from the effects of sleep deprivation and can improve your productivity. You can try it out and see how much better you will feel. Just don't nap too much because it might mess with your sleep cycle, making it difficult for you to fall asleep at night. Be careful but enjoy it!

- Sometimes, it's just doing nothing

Sometimes, rest does not involve any kind of activity. It just involves doing nothing, whether hanging out on the beach, swimming in a pool, taking a walk, or sitting in a given place. You can also practice meditation. Sit quietly in a given space and simply observe your surroundings. Just looking at things and staring out into space may seem like a waste of time and energy, but the thing is, resting contributes to your productivity. And you don't need to be productive every hour of the day. Instead, you should try to find moments where you can recharge your energy. Many times that is by spending time alone, especially for introverts.

- Do some restful activities, such as walking the dog or writing in your journal

Another thing you can do is find restful activities that don't involve too much thinking or reflection. That includes walking the dog or writing in your journal. It helps you externalize your feelings, and it makes you feel better and more energized afterward because you are not focused on the things that you must do. Instead, you choose this kind of activity. You have done it because you want to, not because it's on your to-do list. It is something that will give you genuine joy, and you carry that joy with you no matter where you go.

- Spend time with a few good friends

Depending on your personality, socializing can either be an energizing experience or a draining one. However, most people think that it can be inherently helpful to spend time with a few good friends, playing some ball, watching a movie, or even traveling together. That can be a very restful time for everyone involved. You will see how much better you feel when you can spend a good time with your close friends. The rest will be fantastic.

Be Kind to Yourself

Sleep Tight

Problems with quality of sleep appear both as a result of having anxiety and depression as well as causes in early childhood. Depression and anxiety affect sleep in numerous ways that most often go undetected until they become problematic. The lack of ability to doze off and stay asleep, nightmares, sleep paralysis, and difficulty getting out of bed as a result of poor-quality sleep are the most common sleep problems among those who are suffering from depression. While a lack in the quality of sleep may slow down your progress, you should do the best you can to address this problem and make sure you are getting as much rest as you need.

Here are what you can do to improve your sleep:

- Try to follow a sleep schedule: Think about your daily routine and the most desirable time to go to bed and wake up. Come up with an ideal schedule for going to bed and getting up. If you're having trouble falling asleep, you may have difficulty sleeping according to your schedule. This shouldn't alarm you because your schedule aims at building a healthy habit instead of being instantly effective. Here are a number of ways for you to practice your sleep schedule:

- Don't force yourself to fall asleep: Understand that whether or not you will fall asleep is out of your control. Acknowledge that you can't force yourself to fall asleep. Trust your body's sleep cycle and acknowledge that you will fall asleep when your body and mind feel ready to fall asleep.

- Be consistent with the time that you wake up every morning: Regardless of whether or not you managed to fall asleep the past night, be persistent in getting up every morning around the same time. If this is difficult for you, one of the ways to motivate yourself to get up in the morning is to have scheduled activities. Knowing that you have to be somewhere at a particular time will further motivate you to get off your bed even if you don't feel like it.

- Take sleep seriously: Avoid napping during the day or using your bedroom and bed for activities other than sleep. What you are attempting is to get your body and mind adjusted to associate your bed with sleep and nothing else.

- Change your way of thinking about sleep: While acknowledging that your sleep problems are a result of ongoing health issues, avoid trying to force yourself to fall asleep in any way shape or form. Ironically, the less you worry about sleep, the more you will be likely actually to fall asleep and stay asleep. While it is alright for you to research sleep problems and get educated on the topic, don't turn your efforts into an obsession. The more anxiety present around sleep, the more difficult it will be for you to relax and fall asleep.

Healthy Sleeping Habits

While there is no quick fix with insomnia in depression and anxiety, there are numerous common-sense tips to upsurge your chances of healthy sleep and overall well-being.

Chapter 11:

Social Anxiety Disorder and How to Deal with it

Most people enjoy getting together at social events, meeting new people, dining out, or participating with their team presenting a new client campaign to upper management. These situations are easy and normal for anyone who doesn't have social anxiety.

However, people who live with a social anxiety disorder are not happy that they have this type of disorder. Meeting new people, social events, or even be a participant in a team presentation can cause a wave of anxiousness and fear that can be crippling.

Living with this type of disorder is extremely debilitating, disheartening and can lead to side effects that can only exacerbate the condition. Finding help and relief can offer a positive difference for a person with SAD.

People with SAD have trouble making friends, finding romantic partners, building a career, even attending family events. However, as difficult as this disorder is, there are treatments that are available to help.

Although there is the treatment approach that combines cognitive-behavioral therapy (CBT) and/or medication, SSRIs, there is self-help that can be implemented to help overcome social anxiety.

Effective self-help plans frequently pull from elements of more established approaches. As an example, a self-help plan may integrate exposure to situations a person fears, the reprogramming of thoughts and different types of relaxation methods.

If you have moderate to mild social anxiety, you may feel that you're not able to move forward and trapped. The only way to move forward and release yourself from this feeling is to begin to work towards doing something positive.

Make An Effort To Get Out Into The World

Yes, it's scary and it's much easier to side-step social situations. However, if you suffer from SAD, the most important thing you can do for yourself is to get out into the world and begin to live. Go out to places that give you an uncomfortable feeling, accept invitations, and meet new people.

While you begin to get out and about, you need to fortify yourself and prepare to handle getting out into the world the right way.

Seek Help

Now is the time to seek help. Putting it off to next week is not an option. Frankly, you need to make a commitment to yourself to work towards moving forward and work through this disorder that doesn't serve you well. Don't wait until you're in crisis. The best thing you can do is make an appointment to see someone – today!

You may feel overwhelmed and have that "where do I begin?" mentality. You can seek help and possibly a reference from your physician.

Taking the first is the hardest but can be the first of many steps you'll take to distance yourself from this debilitating condition.

Get Healthy

Make sure that your health is up to par and that being in poor health is not adding to your anxiety. If you're not in good health, make every effort to improve it.

Do regular exercise routines such as weight training and cardiovascular exercise. Walking even for 20 minutes a day three times a week is a good start. Eat a balanced, healthy diet.

Since your nervous system becomes elevated when you become anxious and stress due to SAD, refrain from drinking caffeinated coffee and sodas, and alcohol. Drink tea, preferably chamomile, to calm your nerves.

If you don't have an exercise plan and are not regularly exercising, begin a program. In order to reduce anxiety and stress and increase positive feelings of well-being, starting an exercise program is a way to achieve this.

Exercising with others can give you the opportunity to practice your social skills in an environment that does not provoke any of the usual fears and is a non-threatening place.

If you don't have the time or resources to make regular exercise classes or join a gym, you can still get your exercising into your day. Taking a walk in your neighborhood or at a nearby park or practicing yoga at home are some options.

You can purchase videos or go to YouTube and find yoga instructors that teach entry level to advance. There are quite a few to choose from.

Write Your Goals Down

Writing down your goals down on paper. Read your goals every day. Having unclear, imprecise goals about what you want to achieve will not be enough. Whether you want to become a first-class tennis player or overcome your symptoms of social anxiety, writing down your goals is important. It makes the goals real and perceptible.

Goal setting is where you learn and set benchmarks of where you are now and where and how you decide you want to end up. Find out how you score by taking a self-assessment quiz to measure the level of your social anxiety. This will give you a sense of where you are right now. You can find a number of social anxiety tests that you can take online.

Later on, after you've begun to feel that you have a better sense of yourself and what you've been doing to improve your social skills, take the assessment quiz again and see if there's been an improvement in your scores.

Don't compare others success to your own. Compare yourself on how you've been doing a week, a month, or a year ago. That is the most important barometer for you to compare yourself to – yourself and your progress.

Keep a Daily Journal

In order to see the strides you've made and how you improve over time, keep a daily journal. You'll recognize when you are falling back into negative-thinking and old avoidance habits when you write about your thoughts and experiences.

Since you've written your goals down, you can cross-check and see how you're doing keeping up with them. Jot down some thoughts about your goals and how you've worked towards meeting each one.

Be honest about whether you've been keeping up with them. If not, think about why you haven't and write it down. Before the week is up, go back and read the reasons why you haven't been keeping on track with your goals, then write down what you will be doing about it.

If you're serious about working towards overcoming your social anxiety or at least get a better handle on it, you need to be honest about the work you put into meeting your goals.

Be Your Own Best Supporter

Collect information and develop your knowledge about SAD so you may be able to make better decisions. No one is going to look out for you any better than you are. Ask for adjustments at school and work if you think it will be helpful. Don't be afraid to fight for yourself. You need to have positive thoughts because you're taking care of yourself and trying to make improvements. Be your own best cheerleader!

Explain to others, in an educated manner what your struggles are and what you are doing to deal with them. People whom you attend school with, or work with will have a better understanding of why you are the way you are.

If you're attending a party and feel the need to take a time out, then do so. You need to be kind to yourself and acknowledge what you can and cannot handle.

Honor Who You Are

Realize that there are challenges you face that are more than others have to. Recognize the accomplishments in your life, no matter how small. There may be days that you will be able to be proud of the fact that you actually left the house.

You may not be a great public speaker, but there are many things in your life that you've accomplished that you can take pride in. Build on those small accomplishments and you'll feel a lot better about yourself.

Social Skills – Practice Them Often

You may have a condition that limits you in speaking with people or in front of a group of them, but there are ways that you can improve on the skills that you do have.

- Making introductions – practice doing this by making good eye contact and remembering names. Learn how to give a compliment. If you're making introductions in a business setting and there is hand-shaking all around, practice having a firm (not bone crushing) handshake. It's a universal sign of being assuredness and strength.

- Be assertive – Many people who have SAD also lack assertiveness. The problem is that you don't allow others the opportunity to meet your needs. Assertiveness is being clear about your wants and needs from others so you can be satisfied. It's not to be confused with being aggressive to go after want.

- Share experiences – If you've already overcome your social anxiety disorder or are in the midst of working towards conquering your condition, your experiences should be shared because they are valuable and pertain to who you are and what you are going through.

You may be surprised that sharing your experiences will help others discover that they are not the only ones who may feel the same way you do or have certain aspects of social anxiety they never realized were affecting them.

Another positive aspect of sharing your experiences is that it will bring awareness to a problem that has been kept in the dark. People don't like to admit they have social anxiety because to others it may seem like a sign of weakness. This is a totally incorrect assumption. It is a mental health condition and has nothing to do with weakness.

It takes a very strong individual to admit to their problems, seek help with them and work at overcoming them. Food for thought.

- Begin to say NO– Do you feel as if you're a pushover? Have you had others make demands on you that are unrealistic that they themselves wouldn't perform? Do you have people who treat you badly, but you don't stand up for yourself or to them because you feel incapable of doing so?

Now is the time to begin learning how to say "No" to the unrealistic requests and become more assertive. Clearly, state that you don't want to do what is being asked of you because it's unrealistic.

If you're spoken to disrespectfully and treated badly, let the other person know that it's unacceptable treatment. State it clearly, without stress or anger, but plainly and tell them not to repeat doing so.

If you don't communicate what you want and need clearly, other people can't guess how you feel or what you're thinking.

- Begin to say YES – Rather than falling into the same social anxiety pattern of saying "NO" to everything, like an invitation to a social gathering, try saying "YES" for a change. If you receive invitations to social gatherings, try accepting them more often. There may be feelings of anxiousness when you first begin to attend these events, but the more you do, the less stress, anxiety and fear you'll feel.

So, the next time an invitation arrives in your email or the team at work invites you to join them for lunch when they grab a bite at the local sandwich shop, give it whirl, make the effort and go!

- Find a support group – Joining a support group, whether it's a weekly meeting outside of the home or an online group, will help you to find support and camaraderie with others who understand what you are going through.

Accept the help the group offers and encourage and help others who struggle as well. You understand what others in the group are going through and offering help to even one other person is an act of kindness that will be paid back to you.

- State that you feel nervous – There isn't a person who hasn't felt a bit nervous when they speak in public. One of the best ways to get over the anxiety about public speaking is to actually acknowledge the group or audience that you're nervous before you begin. It breaks the ice and actually, there are more people in that group or audience who have probably felt exactly the same way when they had to speak publicly.

- Go somewhere new – Is your routine get up, shower, get dressed, commute to the office, work, eat lunch, work some more (throw in the occasional meeting), finish up your work for the day and go home, eat dinner, catch a TV program or two and go off to bed? How about your weekends? Still, shop at the same grocery store, and eat out at the same restaurant for brunch every Sunday?

It's time to cut back on the boring and break up the monotonous routine. Get out and go somewhere new. You may not be able to break up the routine of your work schedule and your commute, but you can break up your weekend routine by going somewhere new.

Try a new restaurant for Sunday brunch and challenge your social anxiety with new surroundings. Discover other parts of your neighborhood that you've been missing. You'll be surprised how a change of scenery can lift up your spirits and help you find a whole new world.

- Get a new outfit – Social anxiety can't be cured by retail therapy, but sometimes buying a new outfit can really make you feel upbeat and give you a new attitude.

Purchase something that's different from what you would normally choose to buy. Perhaps, an accessory that complements the outfit and gives it flair. It can be something that will start conversations with others at your job or people who are meeting you for the first time.

- Work on building friendships (and keeping them) – Friendships are a great thing to have. Although you've struggled with social anxiety disorder, you may be at a point that you're ready to develop a friendship, maybe even two. It's time to work at getting to know someone better and possibly turning that person into a friend.

It may seem a bit difficult at first, but as time passes it will give you a good feeling to see someone at work or in class you are familiar with. Take the lead and offer to get together and go out to dinner, take in a movie, or study for the class you both take and grab a bite afterward. Don't wait for the other person to always do the inviting.

Social anxiety disorder can be a difficult condition to overcome, but if your condition is mild or moderate, there are things you can do to help break yourself free.

Realize that all changes take time and your feelings of fear, stress, and anxiousness will not disappear overnight. But do not feel defeated. If you're willing to work through the rough patches and use some of the techniques and tips suggested, you will see the small but steady steps being made and moving forward.

Right now it's important to begin taking hold of this disorder. Don't worry so much about your goals for the time being. Focus on how you're going to get started, seek help, and celebrate the small steps of progress that you will see once you begin your journey using self-help strategies.

Chapter 12:
Sensitization and Desensitization

T he exposure techniques introduced here like desensitization (done either through fantasy or in the real-world), and more extreme kinds, often in the form of implosion or flooding, can both be helpful for taming unrealistic fears and phobias. Exposure methods are proven techniques that work for problems that range from phobias to more serious problems like flashbacks and PTSD.

Sensitization

Sensitization describes what happens when we learn to associate a feeling, like anxiety, with a particular situation. While this can be useful when your learning has been accurate (a fear of rattlesnakes can for example, be a useful fear), much of this conditioned learning can be unrealistic, and even border on the superstitious. When a Veteran of Afghanistan learns that a loud noise may mean an IED and his buddies are in danger, that learning can directly impact survival in Iraq. But the same learning may not translate to a realistic fear in the USA, and the soldier's reaction many not play as well in Peoria when a car backfires.

This specific example about the vet is called a flashback, but phobias and addictive urges are developed in a very similar manner. Phobias often arise when a situation becomes connected with danger, at least in the limbic system and hippocampus of the person with the phobia. However, when no realistic danger persists, but the anxiety still remains (in spades), then the phobia or unrealistic fear becomes entrenched in a manner that is not helpful. It will remain entrenched until you learn differently.

In such situations, if you become sensitized to a predicament, you still feel that same reaction, even when that fear is actually no longer relevant. After that, being in the same or a similar situation or even thinking about that situation, can leave you feeling anxious, or generate a panic reaction.

For example, if you were riding on the freeway during rush hour, and you were involved in a serious motoring accident, you might develop a phobia about driving, especially about driving on the freeway during rush hour. This could be serious, if you need to drive to get to work, or when you need to take the freeway but won't even consider it.

Desensitization

Psychologists and other therapists have figured out how to help in these situations. Desensitization is the process through which you unlearn the connection between anxiety or fear and the situation that evokes it. For this unlearning to occur, you need to enter into the anxiety provoking situation—which is easier said than done—and relearn a more realistic picture. If there is no subsequent danger, you can then eventually come to recognize (and believe) that there is no longer anything to fear.

Exposure therapy relies upon repetition of new, more accurate learning. If you can repeat a troubling situation (or the fantasied version of it) and no harm comes, the association eventually breaks down (the association is said to be extinguished, like a fire extinguisher). However, you should be forewarned: these intense feelings do not go away without a fight. There is usually at least one moment in this process that the fear escalates, often bigger than it ever was before, as if it wants one last chance to convince you of the horrible danger before it gives up and recedes. If you can learn to hang in there at these times, harrowing as they may feel, once you have learned to ride out one or two of these extinction bursts, success is usually close at hand.

There are basically two ways that you can use exposure techniques, and some clients prefer the scary way (flooding or implosion), and others are temperamentally inclined to take it all a bit more gradually (systematic desensitization).

First, let's talk about the hard way. One of the first examples of this approach was described by Wolpe (1958, 1970) who treated a teenage girl who had become terrified of cars after she was in a very scary accident. Wolpe required the girl to get into the car, and then the hysterical, terrified girl was driven around in that car for several hours. Painful and scary as it was, her anxiety gradually abated, and by the time she was released from the car, she was no longer afraid (not even of Wolpe).

This technique, in its severest form, is known as flooding, and it was introduced and formalized as a behavioral technique by a psychologist named Stampfl (1967). Modern incarnations are techniques often also referred to as in vivo (i.e. live) interventions, where an individual is exposed to the aversive situation, often for a few sessions or even one long several-hour session. This is actually a proven technique, one considered an evidence-based treatment— meaning a treatment form that is proven to work. It seems to work effectively with animal phobias and it is also recognized as an effective intervention for fears associated with obsessions and compulsions. In vivo therapy is not always flooding and can be done more gradually but the more aggressive flooding-type therapies are usually in vivo.

While daunting and not the cup of tea of most therapists (or patients), those who participate in in vivo desensitization by flooding interventions find that hanging out with the fear for a prolonged interval, yet with no adverse consequences, serves to "unlearn" the fear connection, and the anxiety desensitizes rapidly and effectively once the fear habituates. It turns out you can get used to almost anything.

The term systematic desensitization is used to describe a careful, systematic approach to implementing desensitization, typically in a gradual and measured manner. This technique can be done in vivo (live in the real world), or as Joseph Wolpe realized in 1973, much or even all of the therapy can be done in an armchair, using imaginary situations and imagined consequences. If you are looking for self-help techniques to use with your anxiety, these armchair approaches may be a daunting place to begin.

Exposure therapies that are designed to systematically desensitize encourage the individual to take a chance and enter into the feared situation. But while flooding or implosive types of in vivo interventions ask you to grab the bull by the horns, a more gradual approach is preferred by most clients and therapists.

The gradual exposure to a series of situations (individually tailored to be increasingly more anxiety-provoking) is called systematic desensitization. In this approach the client and therapist typically collaborate to develop a hierarchy of anxiety-provoking situations culminating in facing the most feared version of the problem. In the live version of this, the therapist accompanies the client and interacts with the targeted problem, but still gradually.

Systematic desensitization involves three steps.

- First, the client needs to learn how to relax in a neutral situation and become skilled at attaining a deep state of relaxation or grounding. Others may prefer to use self-hypnosis or a guided imagery technique, often with images of a safe place, while still others can use techniques that evoke a relaxation response like progressive muscle relaxation. The key here is to evoke a calm and safe feeling and hold on to those safe feelings while confronting the fearful situations. This safe and calm state is not used as an escape, a mistake many therapists have been known to make. Instead it is used as a means of keeping the feeling in check (described in the third step below). Escape scenarios serve to make the anxiety worse.

- A second step is to generate a hierarchy of related anxiety-provoking situations. This means that you make a list of scenes related to the core fear or anxiety. These scenes must have varying degrees of perceived threat. You then arrange them in order from easiest to the hardest to face.

- In the third step you then work your way through the scenes, staying calm while mastering the easiest situation and moving on to the next hardest scene only when the earlier scenes are found to be manageable. The calm and peaceful state obtained in step one is maintained throughout, and serves to inhibit the anxious feeling, because it is generally true that you can't hold two contradictory feelings simultaneously.

In the live version, you face each situation, starting with the easiest, and once that is mastered, you move on to the next. If you are afraid of driving on the interstate, you might first get comfortable with getting in your car and sitting, then with going around the block, and next a ten minute drive through the neighborhood. By the time you get to the interstate, you might drive for only one exit, but soon you can be driving as much as you like, even in rush hour.

The imagination-driven armchair version works just the same, but you do it all in your mind. Sitting in a comfortable place, you first evoke the sense of peace and calm, and then—in your imagination—face the first and easiest challenge. You, of course, need to have worked out the hierarchy in advance, as making it up on the fly can be hard.

The evidence of treatment success behind the imagination-based version is not as compelling, probably because not everyone has the talent of fantasizing vividly, or for that matter of evoking and sustaining a reliably calm and serene state. I also assume some of that failure comes with less skilled therapists who use the safe imagery or feeling as an escape hatch, thereby building greater anxiety. Again, a competent and experienced therapist can help you develop your hierarchy and navigate the escalation in a way more likely to work effectively.

Medication can sometimes help when combined with desensitization, as you can take a strong anti-anxiety drug and then navigate either an implosive exposure or a more gradual one. One problem with a medication approach is that you might be inclined to attribute the success, if any, to the medication (rather than to yourself) and come to believe that the medication is necessary. Of course, most of the benzodiazepines and some other medications used can be habit-forming. The biggest problem, however, is that when the dose is sufficient, it often makes the anxiety largely inaccessible, and therefore it can be harder to evoke the more frightening scenarios.

Prolonged exposure therapy is a term used for the kind of therapy that the Veteran's Administration (VA) tends to rely on for treatment of veterans who have PTSD. This approach has a lot of research backing up that it works. In Prolonged Exposure Therapy sessions at home as homework and in session with the therapist, the client is encouraged to retell their traumatic experiences in the present tense, gradually desensitizing the fear-laden memories. PTSD, however, whether treated in the manner of the VA or more gradually and comprehensively, typically requires a skilled therapist and generally should not be done in a self-help context.

Some virtual reality modules and games have been developed to provide a more realistic exposure to warlike predicaments without having to go on the battlefield. These computer graphic intensive interventions are usually, for now, prohibitively expensive, at least for providers who would like to use them, but there is some indication that prices may be easing.

Eye Movement Desensitization Reprocessing (EMDR) therapy (Shapiro 2001) does not typically emphasize the exposure therapy component, but it seems to play a central role. EMDR is a technique in which the client is asked to attend to an image, sound, or touch, that the therapist uses to engage both the dominant and non-dominant side of the client's brain, while they attend to a fearful memory. It is frequently used not only for treating trauma but other anxiety disorders. However, in my limited experience with it, especially in dealing with acute trauma, the portion of the technique that involves "noticing" whatever image or thought comes is effective—at least in part—because of the role of exposure.

Chapter 13:
Stop Worrying Other People's Opinions

When social anxiety is at its worst, it becomes all consuming. It could sink you into depths of depression; it could handicap you and force you to in your shells. It may even overflow into parts of your life that aren't social at all. You could begin to doubt yourself in every sphere of life, academically, even at work scenes. For me, I would feel a sense of paranoia sweep over me like an inescapable blanket. I begin to fear that there is a looming embarrassment about to happen, that something about would happen every time. It is a cage. You keep fidgeting and asking these questions that further pulls you down. In our society today, it is straightforward to get caught up in thinking about what people think about us.

What do people think about me? How are they judging me? Am I faring well in their eyes? Are they talking negatively about me?

You may not even realize that you're fretting too much. Matter of fact, you may do that so consistently that you may not even recognize the signs of fear because it has become a part of you. These are some of the signs that shows that you worry too much.

1. You're too afraid to talk to others about what you think or believe.

2. If you always think that people around you are upset with you when they aren't.

3. When you do things that you did not plan for it intends to do

and still regret it afterward.

4. If you find it challenging to do something different and maybe even afraid to do so.

5. When you actively avoid certain people, mainly because you are scared that they don't like.

6. You only do what others tell you to do and find it very difficult to make your own decisions.

This damaging self-reflection can lead to nowhere good. So, apply the following strategies to end the anxiety of worrying about what other people think of you. Quit worrying about other people's perception of you and channel that energy into loving yourself more, seeing yourself for who you are and being content with you.

You should stay working to save yourself. It's easier than you realize. The moment you understand and begin to incorporate these eleven (11) philosophies and strategies into your mindset.

Prioritize Your Passion

Take the time to ask yourself what matters in life. Sit and ask yourself what the things matter the most to you are and what things make you happy. In what items do you find happiness and fulfillment? What would you want to define your life? Then figure out what you are compromising to fit into someone else's value system. Weigh your passion against the compromises and sacrifices you are making against your passion and identity so you can fit into other people's scope of interest.

Once you know your values and what drives you – your passion, your interests, your goals and abilities – you'll feel more confident about your everyday actions. Understanding yourself very well will help you be more in your element, and more deliberate and intentional in your decisions. That's because everything you say and do will be backed by purpose.

For example, you could say, "I strive to be a great father, have a successful career, be a moral and generous person, etc." Use goals to initially define your passion lay out goals that would help you achieve your love and then expand your vision to form a complete picture of who you are or who you want to be.

When you feel confident about what you value and prioritize, you'll instinctively put those values above someone else's negative opinions.

It's Not All About You

The truth is that most people are anxious about themselves, not you. Most people's outbursts and treatment of others are just an extension of how they feel about themselves. Think about it, when you walk into a crowded room or a public social setting, aren't you primarily focused on your actions and well-being? The way you react and respond to other people, is it not an extension of how you feel within yourself?

Well, pretty much everyone else has that same way of thinking. Everyone is internalizing their self while in a social setting and using it to affect other people. They're not analyzing you under a microscope. If anything, they are more concerned with what's happening to them and how you and everyone else perceives them.

I'm not trying to take you down a peg by breaking this news to you.

But you're not as much in the limelight as you may think. Imagine walking down the road; I bet you imagine everyone else looking at you, watching your steps and how you carry yourself. You believe everyone is holding a microscope against you and watching you in every detail. But it is not so. Life is not so. You are barely noticed.

In some ways, this gives you the upper hand because you know people are concerned primarily with themselves, and you can play to that to better orchestrate a positive, fulfilling social dynamic. More on that in a bit.

Sticks and Stones May Break My Bones

Remember that nursery rhyme you learned as a kid: "Sticks and stones may break my bones, but words can never hurt me"? Well, it still holds as an adult.

Negative opinions about you can't hurt you unless you digest them, mull over them, and let them hurt you. You have to permit those opinions to hurt you as strange as that may sound. You have to give these opinions the audience and stage to grow and bear down on you. Now, from time to time, it's possible that people may have negative views about you for whatever reason best known to them. You should know that those opinions come from one of two places. Either the person on the other side is insecure about their self and is throwing out negativity as a defensive mechanism or their opinion is valid.

If there is some validity to the opinion, try to take the information and treat it objectively. Decide for yourself if the view is valid or just the tantrum of a troubled individual. Don't just take anything someone says to you or about you as the truth. Process what was said and determine if it's worth your consideration.

Remember, you have the power to let words and opinions affect you. Choose to keep all feedback as constructive or dismiss it as a problem that rests with the other party involved.

Letting Go

You have no control on what they think, and in this light, your mantra needs to be, "You can't worry about what you can't control." Let go of the things you can't control, and let go of the things that are above your abilities.

If you do worry about what you can't control, you're going to instantly increase your anxiety by exposing yourself to a factor that's bound to sting sooner or later. You would keep yourself stagnant and immobile, unproductive.

It's crucial that you understand most social judgment, finger pointing and criticism comes from a place of insecurity on the part of the accuser.

Leave it at that and let the negative opinion be their problem, not yours. Carry yourself with high esteem and walk away from unconstructive criticisms that are coming from a place of insecurities.

You need to move on and focus on the positive, focus on your values, and find comfort in knowing that you act in a way that's aligned with your belief system. And feel safe with the realization that you know where you are going, and it is where you want to go. Embrace yourself and let go of everything else.

Look More Outward

Internalizing your judgment makes you your own worst critic. All social anxiety is just your own internalized perception. You look at your actions with such granular detail that you pick apart every little thing that in reality goes unnoticed by those around you. Cut it out! Try to look more outward at what you want, and expect and value rather than falling into the habit of internalizing and drawing inward. It will help you be more active in the social setting around you and allow you to leave your inhibitions behind.

Think About Why You Care

Many times, we worry too much because of what social norms have inculcated in us. In this our time, we are being instructed to dress a certain way, act a certain way, and even live a certain way. The popular belief of individuals is that anything that strays from the "norm" is too different.

Because of this belief, it can make us start to worry and develop a fear of being judged by others. Try to recognize what makes you care and what you should care about so you can understand it better.

When you know that it is not your fault and nothing is wrong with you, you'll understand that the society we live in has a role to play in the developed fear of rejection or judgment. Once you recognize this, you'll find it easier to start accepting yourself.

Be Focused on Being in The Moment

It is always easier to stop worrying about things and focus on what's happening now when you are living in the present. Instead of thinking

"I like this outfit, and it looks lovely on me, what if people judge me for wearing it?", you would be thinking, "I love this dress and it's awesome."

You will not focus your energy on what might happen because it is something you will be able to control. Try to channel your energy on the moment and accept yourself for who you are. Refrain from bothering about the "could" and "ifs" of the future. Once you do all this, it will be very much more comfortable to stop worrying about anybody judging you.

Know That People Don't Normally Care

All through our lives, most of the time, our focus is only on ourselves. This scenario is typical for everyone, including those you believe must be judging you. People go through life worrying about what others think when those people may not be judging you or anyone else. Realize that everyone has their own lives and things to deal with. Their thinking will be about themselves and not other people.

When you leave your house, you may worry that people will judge you based on how you're dressed or act. It may surprise you, but most everyone is thinking the same thing. A lot of us do not worry about what others are wearing or doing.

Once you realize that other people have their insecurities and worries, it will be easier to stop worrying so much about what people think.

Practice Self-Love and Acceptance

An essential thing to remember when talking about worrying too much is that you have to love yourself first before anything or anyone else. Constantly worrying about what others think shows that you have very little self-confidence and low self-esteem.

When you practice self-care by showing self-love, you will not worry too much about what others think. Self-care can be done through meditation, spending time with nature, eating healthy, etc. Whatever it is that brings you joy is enough and make sure you show yourself you love every day.

Although it may take a while when you perfect the act of loving yourself, you can stop worrying so much and accept yourself for who you are. And you don't need anyone's approval!

Find Your Group of People

When you are around people who lift you up and help you feel positive, it helps you to stop worrying about others. People who care about you will emphasize your strengths and the positive things about you that you may not even know. This intervention can help you on your path to self-acceptance.

When you have a close group of friends who are positive and honest, it will help because you can ask questions whenever you feel like others are judging you, and they will be truthful and accurate.

When you talk to your friends about your worries, they will point out the good in you and help you to start feeling more confident.

Understand That You Can't Please Everyone

Whatever decision or action you take in this life, one thing you should bear in mind is that you cannot please everyone. It is an impossible task. There always will be people who are judgmental toward you. It's just how they are wired. Even if people do judge you for something, they mostly never act on it or react by confronting you. It's just a thought that pops up in their head.

People who matter to you will probably never judge you while those who do may not matter at all. The earlier you accept the fact that you can't please everyone and that people will judge you no matter what, especially if that's their character, you will receive it and work on not worrying much.

Conclusion

With the strategies and techniques provided in this book, you now have the means to defeat your anxiety. It's just up to you now to use what you have been shown. You can get out of your chair, stand up and shout "screw your anxiety, I'm in control now!" Or you lie there, feeling sorry for yourself and say "never-mind, I guess what will be will be". Choose either one, but remember one thing…our time on this earth is finite, and the longer you allow anxiety to rule your life, the longer you miss out on the great times you could have.

Address the root cause, then move on to building up your confidence and self-esteem. Move on to managing your panic attacks through breathing exercises and agitator management. Finally, don't be afraid to tackle your anxiety head on and conquer it. Never be afraid to understand your anxiety. As the saying goes, "Keep your friends close, but your enemies closer."

Anxiety is a disease; it can be cured but sometimes it takes a little more work than others. Treat yourself in the same manner as you will treat a loved one with the same affliction. If you were in charge of giving them support to overcome their anxiety, what would you do?

The first step in beating anxiety is admitting that you have this condition and it needs to be treated. The second step is seeking help from the experts who have gone through similar experiences/ The third and final step is to take action against your condition by implementing what you've learned from the prior two steps.

After all that's done, you will be almost there. It can take a while, but in the end, being around your family and friends will seem like heaven on earth.

 The history of anxiety disorders goes back to the times of the Ancient Greeks. It was described as being an "unpleasant or unpleasant experience". It is an emotion now considered normal and human, but there are those who struggle with it, and that is where the real issue begins.

Remember that you are not alone. Many people understand what you are going through. Even if people don't, let them help you and never be afraid to ask. You don't ever have to be alone in this life. Reach out and ask.

All the best, and I wish you an anxiety-free life.